T0368096

REMOVE THE LOCK

BECOME PERMANENTLY FREE

RICHARD KIRBY PAYNE

WESTBOW
PRESS®
A DIVISION OF THOMAS NELSON
& ZONDERVAN

This book is a work of non-fiction. Unless otherwise noted, the author and the publisher make no explicit guarantees as to the accuracy of the information contained in this book and in some cases, names of people and places have been altered to protect their privacy.

WestBow Press books may be ordered through booksellers or by contacting:

WestBow Press
A Division of Thomas Nelson & Zondervan
1663 Liberty Drive
Bloomington, IN 47403
www.westbowpress.com
844-714-3454

Scripture quotations are from the ESV® Bible (The Holy Bible, English Standard Version®), copyright © 2001 by Crossway, a publishing ministry of Good News Publishers. Used by permission. All rights reserved.

ISBN: 979-8-3850-4336-1 (sc)
ISBN: 979-8-3850-4335-4 (e)

Print information available on the last page.

WestBow Press rev. date: 02/19/2025

CONTENTS

Part 5: Alone Again

INTRODUCTION

It's hard to live your whole life and not wonder if you've missed something important along the way. Some things I want to remember. Some things I want to forget.

There are plenty of things that I did that I would gladly forget. I don't want to feel guilty or responsible for things that didn't turn out well, and I don't want other people to find out about them. If I tell my story, they might forget or only remember the parts they want to remember. However, if I write down all the details, anyone can read and reread what happened in my life. Then where am I?

When a friend asked me to write a book about my experience of losing my wife after thirty years, I had no idea what it would become. What was I supposed to include in the book? What was I supposed to talk to somebody about possibly including in the book? What did I want to remember and what did I want to forget? Would any of these things help anybody who is going through a similar situation in their life?

I wrote the book. I didn't do what my friend suggested. She wanted me to only think about writing the book. She said there would be a time in the future when I would be ready to share my experiences. She gave me a great idea, so I went with it. However, I didn't wait.

I started writing children's stories before my wife died. I continued after she died. While I was writing the children's stories, I began the book about how a person's soul could survive the loss of their precious mate. I will include some of that in this book as well.

Long before I considered writing children's stories, I was an author. I loved to write poems. I still do. I loved to write things about my life. I still do. People call them memoirs. I decided that a better word was chronicles. There are a lot of things that I never wrote. There are a lot of things that my friends wish I never wrote but I did.

My chronicles started when I graduated from high school. In 1977, computers were beginning to become available to normal people, but I still wrote in journals. The problem is you can easily lose a journal. Or it can get wet. Or your dog can eat it.

Fortunately for me, and maybe you, I didn't have a dog. I was careful about handling the journals. They didn't get wet or lost. I packed a lot of stuff when I moved. Now, I like the flexibility and safety of having multiple electronic copies of my work, so I use a computer.

I consolidated and organized my chronicles. I have a printed copy in a notebook. It has about 150 typewritten pages. I couldn't find the copy that was on a computer. I was nervous that I might lose them, so I entered my chronicles into a Microsoft Word document. As I was entering them, I did minimal editing.

My chronicles cover the time between high school graduation and when I married my wife in 1993. A lot has happened since 1993. This book will include some of those events and my thoughts, along with my chronicles.

No good story starts in the middle, so I start my story when I was born. I don't remember much of my early life. Anything that I can remember must be important to my story.

I need a name for this book. One of the things that I think about before I go to bed is the security of my house. I always check to see if my front door is locked. It would be a rare event for it not to be locked. I live in a safe neighborhood. I check the front door anyway. I wonder why.

This was a rough week for me. Today is a day to relax. Several times today, I stood from my easy chair to exercise. I walked around the house and thought of something to do. When I went by the front door, I checked to see if it was locked. It's in the middle of the afternoon, so there's no reason for me to check it but I did. I asked why, but nobody answered my question.

My front door has a peephole. When I check to see if the front door is locked, I also look out the peephole to see if there's anything on the front porch. I often forget if I'm scheduled to receive a delivery. I don't want something sitting on the front porch all night, even if no one will steal it.

There are a lot of uncertainties in my life. I'm excited but also nervous. I shouldn't be nervous but I am. There are many things that can change the trajectory of my future. I believe good things are in store for me. The things that have already happened are not going to change. They're locked in place. The only thing left to do with them is evaluate them. Do I want to learn something from my experiences or do I want to try to eliminate them from my memory? For everything that is in this book, you can conclude the category that they belong in.

I learned a lot of things from my experiences. Maybe you have learned from your experiences too. As I share my experiences, I will include commentary. Perhaps you can learn from my experiences. There is no extra charge for that.

PART I

The Early Days

CHAPTER 1

What Child Is This?

I was born in 1959 in Parkersburg, West Virginia. My brother, Robert, was two years old. My dad was a chemical engineer for DuPont. When I was five months old, my family moved to Wilmington, Delaware. My dad worked in the plastics facility. They say if you work for DuPont and you ever get transferred to Wilmington, you will never leave. Some people think DuPont owns the whole state, but it doesn't.

We stayed in Wilmington. Even after he retired, my dad lived near Wilmington. My mom died when I was nineteen years old. She is buried in a cemetery close to the city. When my dad died, we buried him with my mom.

Our first house in Wilmington had three bedrooms in a quiet neighborhood. My best friend lived next door to us. His brother was the same age as Robert. We did a lot of things together. We were soldiers, Indians, bikers, and just kids who ran around, played in the dirt, and got in trouble. But not too much trouble.

My friend Andy was small like me. His brother, Johnny, could take care of himself—and us too. There wasn't any reason to be concerned, but it was nice having a friend who could take care of me. Just his presence was sufficient. I was glad that he was my friend instead of my enemy.

It was hard when Andy and Johnny moved to New Jersey. We

thought we would stay connected by sending notes in the mail. I'm not sure what happened. We just stopped sending letters. Why do we lose connection with our friends? It is rare to stay connected with childhood friends.

My family called me Ricky. My brother wanted to be called Robert. Our grandmother made Christmas stockings using these names.

When I was five years old, I decided that Ricky was a name for a little boy. I didn't think I was a little boy. I talked to my parents. My dad said, "Do you want to be called Rick?"

I said, "I like that name." People started calling me Rick. Even after I was grown, my sister continued to call me Rick. I was OK with that. Rick is a neat name. When she was young, if Sherry wasn't sure about something, she would say, "I will go ask Rick."

Somewhere along the way, my name changed from Rick to Rich. From that point on, my friends called me Rich. I was still Rick to anyone who knew me when I was a child. When I introduce myself, I say my name is Richard, even though everybody calls me Rich. I wonder why I do that.

My dad could do anything and fix anything. He built things with wood, fixed electrical and plumbing problems, and painted. He made a multiple-level flower bed in the backyard using bricks. He grew up on a farm, so he knew a lot about growing vegetables. My dad took Robert and me fishing in his small rowboat that he carried on top of his car. He bought a used bicycle for me. He took the bike apart and painted it black. Then he put it back together. I liked the bike after it was painted.

My dad tried to teach me everything he knew. I remember a lot, but not much transferred into useful skills. Of the things my dad taught me how to do, I think painting is the only one that I do well.

My dad loved to play golf. I wondered why he played so much. He played with his customers. One of his products was used to make golf balls, so they tested the golf balls. My dad loved to go fishing with his customers. One of his products was used to make fishing lines, so they tested the fishing line.

One of my dad's customers gave him an expensive bowling ball. It was made from one of my dad's products. Since he didn't bowl, he gave it to me for Christmas. That was a great present!

I told my dad that I wanted a job like his so I could be paid to have fun. I couldn't find that kind of job.

My dad helped one of his friends get elected as a state representative. That was cool. We got a lot of things with names of people who were running for office. We were asked to pass them out in our neighborhood. Robert and I rode our bikes around the neighborhood and handed out whistles, combs, and things like that. A boy came out to the street to meet us and asked how much he could buy with the five dollars he just earned. He didn't know what we had, but he wanted to buy some. We told him that the things were free. He called all his friends, and we gave away everything we had.

One day, I came home from school and saw a For Sale sign in front of our house. I asked, "When are we going to move? Where are we going to move? Why are we going to move?"

Dad said, "We are not moving."

That was confusing to me, so I asked, "Why is there a 'For Sale' sign in front of our house?"

Dad said, "We don't own this house. We rent. The people who own the house want to sell it, and they gave us an opportunity to buy it. They had to put the sign in the front yard anyway."

I never understood it.

My friends thought we were going to move. I told them we were not. They didn't understand either.

My dad and mom bought the house, and we didn't move.

When I was almost five, my sister was born. It was cramped in our house. Robert and I shared a bedroom. Baby Sherry got her own room. Robert and I had fun times in our room. We got an old blanket and made a tent.

When my parents bought a window air conditioner, it came in a huge box. They put the box on the driveway. My friends and I used the box as a fort.

When Sherry started to walk, she had a baby and a baby carriage. She said, "My baby wants to go for a walk."

I was responsible for watching my little sister. I said, "I think your baby is tired and wants to go to sleep."

Sherry said, "She wants to go for a walk."

I walked with Sherry and her baby in the baby carriage. I was learning to be a dad even at a young age.

After college, I moved away from home. Because I was lonely, I wrote a poem to remember what it was like when I was young. This is the only poem of mine that was published.

Little Froggies
July 31, 1985

I think of little froggies
And blankets on the bed;
I think of little doggies
And bikies in the shed.

I think of little kitties
And ball games in the yard;
I think of little mitties
And hearties on the card.

I think of little boaties
And splashing in the pool;
I think of little coaties
And workies with the tool.

I think of little mommies
And daddies hugging tight;
I think of little sissies
And bobbies through the night.

I had some neat friends in our neighborhood. The boys were younger than me, but I still had a good time. All summer long, I played cards with my friend Bobby on his front porch. When we finished each day, he did not bring the cards into his house. He put them in the mailbox on his front porch. He knew that we would play with them again the next day.

There were two girls my age who lived across the street. I liked them, and they were pretty. I walked with one to school for a few years.

When I was ten, my parents bought a larger house so that my grandmother could live with us. The new house was in a newly developed neighborhood. There were only a few trees. The builders put sod down in our yard. They dug up a large rock and left it in our front yard. I asked my dad why they left it. He said that it had character and looked good.

My dad had a friend who owned a farm. He gave us small trees to plant in our yard. It was a lot of fun helping plant them. Every time we dug a hole, we found junk. The builders needed more landfill so they used junk.

My dad put trees in the backyard. They were the right distance to hang a hammock. My dad loved to lie on a hammock. When I tried, I fell off. After many years, the trees grew and created so much shade that the grass died in the backyard. Sadly, we removed a few of the trees.

I missed my friends from the old neighborhood, but I made new friends. My two best friends lived on my street.

My friend across the street had a friendly dog. It was the most obedient dog I've ever seen. There was no fence around their yard, and the dog never ran away. One day, the dog was excited when she saw my cat. The dog chased my cat. My friend's dad was in the front yard and called the dog. As soon as he called the dog, it turned around and went home. I was amazed. After that, my cat was more careful.

5

CHAPTER 2

Why Am I Here?

I was still young when I started asking, "Why am I here?" I wasn't looking for the answer to a philosophical question. I wanted to know what I could do to contribute. I wanted to contribute to my family, my church, my neighborhood, and my school. I didn't think I had to contribute everywhere at the same time. I was trying to figure out what I was good at.

Some kids were athletic. One of my friends was on the baseball team and the soccer team. He played goalie. In one of the games, he got hurt and had to stay home for a few weeks. I brought schoolwork to him. One day, I asked him, "When you get better, are you still going to be on the soccer team?"

He said, "Sure. Why not?"

I thought of a few reasons, but he didn't want to know any of them.

I had another friend who wanted to be an Air Force pilot. His dad was a pilot. It sounded scary to me. I guess he became a pilot. He also had a motorcycle. Robert and I wanted to ride on his motorcycle with him, but my mom was concerned that we would get hurt. We never rode on his motorcycle.

I had another friend who wanted to be a park ranger. I didn't know what that was.

I had another friend who was a good chess player. He was the best chess player in our school and the captain of the chess team. When he graduated high school, he was planning to go to an expensive out-of-state school. He had good grades. After I graduated high school, I was riding to the University of Delaware on a bus. When I saw my friend, I was surprised because I thought he got a scholarship. I guess he didn't. When I asked him what classes he was taking, he said, "A little of this and a little of that." I was sad, but I didn't know what to say or do.

I had another friend in high school who liked to play chess, but he wasn't good. He was a gambler. He asked to borrow a few dollars from me in the morning. In the afternoon, he paid me back. I thought, "He must be gambling at school." I never asked him because I didn't want to know.

One day when we were eating lunch, he asked to play chess with me. He said, "Let's play for five dollars."

I said, "I'm the best chess player in the school now." That was after several good chess players had graduated. I could defeat my friend without even looking at the pieces. I said that I would play with him, but I wasn't going to gamble. He was disappointed, but he was still my friend.

I had another friend for several years. She was nice, but I wasn't attracted to her. She was on the planning committee for the senior prom. I guess she didn't have a date. One of the teachers who knew us well came to me privately and asked if I wanted to go to the prom with her. They offered to help me financially. They thought that that was the only reason I didn't ask her. I told the teacher that was generous, but I wasn't interested in going to the prom.

I enjoyed helping people. I decided to be a math tutor while I was in high school. I talked to a person at school who helped find part-time jobs for students. He set me up with students in my school and other schools. Most of the students I tutored were not motivated. The tutoring sessions did not last long because their parents didn't want to continue to pay me.

I helped a young girl across the street when she was trying to learn her multiplication tables. She didn't think she needed help, but her mom asked me to help. The girl didn't like my style of tutoring. That didn't last long.

For Student Leadership Day, my calculus teacher asked me if I would be the teacher for her class. That was a huge challenge since I was attending the class that she wanted me to teach. She said she didn't have anybody else who could do it. She knew I was interested in becoming a teacher. I decided to take her up on it. She said I did a good job of leading her class.

A chemistry teacher asked me to be her lab assistant. I had already taken chemistry. The kids in the class called me Mr. Chemistry. I thought that was funny.

Halfway through my senior year, one of the math teachers told me that the school installed a computer terminal. It was connected to a University of Delaware computer. He had some information about programming, but there wasn't a class available at our high school. I told him I wanted to learn by myself, so he gave me the information and a log-in to the computer.

I went to my calculus teacher and asked her if I could demonstrate to the class how computers can be used to solve math problems. She told me to go ahead. I created the program and demonstrated it to my class. The students were amazed. My teacher was amazed. I was amazed that it worked.

I did more things on the computer. I created a program that played chess and other board games. I was hooked. It was obvious to everyone.

When I was considering graduation, I knew I was going to the University of Delaware, but I wasn't sure what major to choose. Originally, it was going to be education. I investigated the potential jobs in education and computer science. A bachelor's degree in computer science could draw a typical salary that was 50 percent more than a master's degree in education. I talked with one of my teachers. He said that if I wanted to go into education, it would be a good career, but I needed to realize it was going to be rough. He told me he wasn't doing well financially.

It was hard for me to make the decision to change from education to computer science. I thought my purpose in life was to be an educator—to help children and to make a difference in high school. With a degree in education, I wouldn't make enough money to support a family. It was sad. People who potentially could have the greatest impact on the next generation were not properly compensated.

I didn't want to be poor, but I also did not give up on education. My plan was to get a bachelor's degree in computer science and find a good job. Then I would go for my master's in something that would combine education and computers. The University of Delaware had a good program. I didn't finish my master's degree, but I had opportunities later in my career to use what I learned about education.

Now that I am retired, my interest in helping children is renewed. I started writing children's books. I know there are other things that will help fulfill my dream. Reviewing the events of my life will reveal hidden talents and passions.

CHAPTER 3

An Invisible Door

This was my dream.

I was walking through the country in the middle of the night. It was dark and there were no stars. I could not see the moon. It was difficult walking through the tall grass and weeds. I approached an old house that was not maintained. It wasn't ready to fall, but I couldn't imagine that anybody was living there.

There was a rail fence around most of the yard. I approached the house from the front. I opened the gate and walked on the path toward the front door.

I didn't know why I was drawn to the house. I felt like I was trespassing, but who would know that I was there? I slowly opened the front door. I expected to hear a squeaking sound like in a scary movie, but the door opened easily with no sound.

When I walked inside the house, I wasn't surprised. It continued to give me the impression that nobody had been in the house for a long time. The house was fully furnished, but there were no personal items. Everything was dusty and I felt cobwebs. I wasn't sure how I could see anything, but dreams are like that.

I walked up the stairs and looked in the bedrooms. They were fully furnished as well, with sheets, blankets, and pillows on the beds.

When I entered one of the bedrooms, I was frightened. It

appeared that there was a large person lying on the bed underneath the bedding.

I slowly exited the room and quietly closed the door. I went down the stairs and out the back door as quickly as I could without making noise. The backyard looked like the front, with one exception—there was a wire mesh on the rail fence. I wondered if I was going to be able to get through the fence or if I would have to leave through the front yard.

I saw a small opening in the fence. I quickly went through the opening. I was glad to be off the property.

As I turned around to look at the house, I thought I might see the person from the bedroom coming after me. Instead, I saw a young lady who was fully dressed. I wondered if she lived in the house or was trying to escape.

It was still dark, but I could see an amazing number of details.

The young lady looked at me with a sad face. I continued to look at her for a few minutes. I expected her to say something, wave at me, or turn around and leave. She stood still and continued to stare at me. I felt that she was telling me to leave and pretend like I had not been there.

I turned around and walked away from the house. There was a small creek that I could easily step over. I kept walking toward what looked like a river in the distance.

When I woke, I sat on the side of my bed and wondered if I should write down the dream. The dream was so vivid that I thought I would never forget it. I haven't.

In preparation for writing this chapter, I thought about this dream. As I was writing, I remembered all the details. I felt the pain from the young lady again. I can still see the sad look that was on her face. She wanted to leave, she was ready to leave, but she couldn't.

Our church hosted a Christian school. There were several rooms that were locked to protect the lab equipment. My dad told me that someone had picked the locks. When the rooms were checked, it did not appear that anything was stolen or damaged, but it was obvious that someone had been in the rooms.

Better locks were placed on the doors, but that did not stop the break-ins. When they finally verified who was doing it, they tried to counsel the boy, but he did not change. My dad said to me that he thought that there was not a lock that existed in the world that this boy could not break into.

I was still young, so my dad didn't tell me a lot. It was hard for me to believe that my friend was doing this, but I knew that there was sufficient evidence against him.

I thought he should find a job in security. His knowledge would be valuable for people who want to make better locks.

As the boy grew, things did not get better for him. His father had a high-paying job and probably could've sent him to any school that he wanted to go to. Unfortunately, the boy rejected help from his parents. He finally got a job with a construction crew, got married, and had children. Trouble continued to follow him.

He wasn't the only one. There were others that I knew struggled. Their life was like the old abandoned house in my dream. It didn't fall, but it was obviously not taken care of. Everything that was needed was available. There was something hidden that was keeping these people trapped. It was like an invisible door with a lock. The reason the lock could not be opened was because the door could not be found.

When I started to realize my desire to help children, I felt like I was not only inadequate but also unaware of the traps that these children were in. I was afraid to make an effort to understand how to help them.

CHAPTER 4

To Be or Not to Be?

You can't give something that you don't have. I wanted to show my friends how they could become free, but I was struggling to become free myself. Each person must deal with their prison cell. I was not hurting people or breaking into locked rooms, but I wanted friends to accept me the way I was.

Was I allowed to be myself or did I have to become somebody else? Did I need to be a little more normal than I was?

When I was in kindergarten, we had a game during recess. The girls chased the boys. When a boy was caught, the girl was allowed to kiss him. The boys didn't like to be kissed by a girl. They wanted to run around, get dirty, and play with bugs. I liked doing those things, but I also liked making friends. I saw no reason why a friend couldn't be a girl. If she wanted to give me a kiss out of friendship, I wasn't going to stop her.

Every year, the girls became prettier. Their hair shined in the sunlight. They were sweet and enjoyed my company. I wrote short poems that rhymed. I included words that made my friends feel special. The older I got, the better my poems became.

I'm introducing this early because I started early. This will be a reoccurring theme throughout my book. Some things were obvious in the early part of my life. Other things were just hinted at.

Along with my tendency to be creative was a form of pride. I

13

also had a tremendous imagination. Like wanting to be Superman or one of the Avengers, I wandered into a daydream that made me feel better than everybody.

We did not visit my cousins often because they lived down South. Whenever we visited them, we drove in our car. It was a long way to Louisiana and Texas. We treasured those vacations because we didn't get them often.

On one visit, Robert and I were playing with our cousin, Cindy, and her friends in the yard next door. Even though I was a friendly person, I was insecure when I was around kids that I didn't know.

The neighborhood kids suggested new games to play. Whoever suggested the game had to explain it. I wasn't sure I wanted to do that, but I was bored with the games that they were playing. Cindy discerned that I had a game I wanted to suggest, but she could see that I was holding back. I started to explain the game, but then I stopped.

One of the older kids thought I was inferring that they couldn't understand how to play my game because they weren't smart enough. Cindy could see that things weren't going so well, so she intervened.

Cindy said, "You're just an ordinary boy. You're nothing special. Just tell us how to play the game."

I knew that Cindy was trying to be loving, but it didn't come off that way.

I explained the game. The kids liked it and even made a few adjustments so that the younger kids would be able to compete with the older ones.

Later, I started replaying the interaction in my mind. I often did that when I felt like people didn't understand me. I was trying to find a way to justify what I did. Most of the time I didn't. It made me more frustrated and sometimes even angry, but I didn't let anybody know that.

All during grade school, I pretended to be somebody I was not. I did not like playing games where people got hurt, but I joined in when my friends wanted to play tackle football at recess. I wasn't a big guy, but I played anyway.

CHAPTER 5

Young Blood

The Red Jackets

One of the first ministries that I got involved in at my church was being an usher. I didn't know it at the time, but it was to be a lifelong ministry that would open many doors for other opportunities to serve the Lord.

I was first asked to be an usher at the age of fourteen. Our church leaders encouraged the youth to get involved, and being an usher was not difficult as well as teaching responsibility. The head usher put Brian and me on the balcony where we couldn't mess up too badly since there were only four rows.

After a while, we were permitted to usher in the main section of the sanctuary. That was a privilege for me, although I am not sure that staying on the balcony wasn't preferred by my friends. At one time, there were four teenage boys involved in ushering. We were best friends and we did a lot of things together. That is probably how we decided to usher together.

My dad called us the Four Musketeers. We had an "all for one and one for all" attitude.

We each had a red sports jacket. They were fashionable at the time, and sometimes we wore our red jackets to usher. Some of the other ushers had red jackets too.

One Sunday morning, we had a guest speaker. He noticed that both ushers on the balcony were wearing red jackets. Also, I was downstairs on one side and another usher with a red jacket was on the other side. Although we had not planned it, we looked symmetrical and professional-looking, with the corners having an usher with a red jacket. The guest speaker thought that they were uniforms for the ushers.

The red jackets were a sign of the times for my friends. We did lots of things together, like staying up all night to play Monopoly and watching old movies.

I recall some questionable things that were suggested by my friends. Fortunately, someone would remember to continue to honor God. Even at that early age, the Lord was working in our lives to be a positive influence on our peers.

In my pile of mementos, I have a pew card that someone drew during that church service. From the artistic likeness of the people and the Spanish words written next to the figures, I can only think of one of my friends. I got out my Spanish-English dictionary to translate the messages that were passed back and forth. If preachers only knew where our thoughts are during their sermons.

Champions

When I was in high school, I loved sports. I played on the church softball team. I was on a bowling team. I played basketball and tennis. I even liked touch football. But I wasn't good at any of these.

I played tennis with Nancy. She was better than me. We stopped when I got tired. I could keep up with her for about one set and then I was done.

I loved playing on the church softball team even though I didn't play much. I sat on the bench and kept the score most of the time. I encouraged my teammates even when things weren't going well. Only guys played in this league. The wives and girlfriends cheered their men on. Linda would always say, "Come on, guys. You can do it!" Most of the time, they did. Her husband was one of the best players on the team. Occasionally, I had a good game, but I wasn't an athlete.

I tried out for the baseball team at school. I didn't make the first cut.

My friend, Brian, and I shot baskets at his house. He was better than me. He had neat trick shots. You stand somewhere on the driveway and turn around. You throw the basketball over your head and it lands in the basket. Swish! If the ball hits the rim or the backboard, it won't go in. For the trick to work, you had to stand in the same place and practice hundreds of times. When somebody came that didn't know about the trick, they were amazed.

I love football. On Thanksgiving morning, some of the guys went to a field next to a school and played touch football. They called it the Turkey Bowl. Originally, it was just the men and boys from a few families. Over time, more people were invited to play. I didn't like sports where people got hurt. That's why I liked touch football instead of tackle.

My church organized a bowling league. I wasn't one of the best, but I had my moments. I had my bowling ball, a bag to put it in, and shoes. I looked like I was a pro. My style was unorthodox, but I could string some strikes together. At other times, I did not play as well.

I played well for one year. I didn't think I would get an award, but I was happy to play my best. It was the last game of the tournament. Everyone didn't play every day. I didn't realize how well I was doing. I wondered why everybody was cheering me on, even people who were not on my team.

In case you're not familiar with the game, I'll put a few details in. The best you can do in any frame is knock all the pins down with one ball. That's called a strike. If you don't get all the pins down with your first ball, you get one more ball. If you get all the pins down with two balls, that's called a spare. When you're scoring your frame, you get one bonus for a spare and two bonuses for a strike.

That night, I didn't realize how well I was doing. It was phenomenal for me and everyone else in our league. At the end of

17

the seventh frame, I had one spare and six strikes in a row. Even if I played my average for the last three frames, I would have an incredibly high score.

Prior to that night, the person with the highest game had a score of 242. I wasn't thinking about getting near that score. The best game for me in that league was 196.

That night was my one chance to be a champion.

I didn't know what was going on anywhere other than my game. I did not talk to people or eat food. I did not walk around while I was waiting for the next person to bowl. I kept my mind on the game.

When I stood up to bowl in the eighth frame, I noticed that someone was sitting in the seats behind my alley. Often, people watched, but why was *he* here? He played his last game the previous week. I thought he was home doing homework, watching a video, or talking to somebody on the phone.

I should not have thought about it, but I did. I knew he was the one with the highest game of 242. Oh no! I was about to make him number two. How could I possibly do that? He was the best bowler in the league. He had many games over 200, so why was he here? I was no threat to him. Or was I?

I attended this church since I was a baby. Everybody knew me. All the longtimers and the newcomers. Everybody liked me. I was a likable person. I tried to be humble, and I was a little bit, but maybe not enough.

Everyone was cheering me on. I looked at the score on the screen above my head before I bowled the eighth frame. There must've been a mistake. I couldn't believe I had that score. I knew I was doing well, but not that well. I couldn't get a perfect game because the first frame was a spare instead of a strike. But this game was going to be *phenomenal*. Everyone was cheering for me.

Almost everyone. The guy sitting in the back who had the 242 game said nothing.

I bowled the first ball and it almost went in the gutter. One point. That was sad, but not too bad. All I had to do was bowl the second ball like it was the first ball. If I got all the pins down, I would have a spare, which would give me more bonus points. I bowled the second ball and it went in the gutter.

When I bowled the ninth and tenth frames, I did a little bit better, but not much. Being nervous kept me from bowling well.

At the end of the game, my score was 222, which was the highest game I bowled in my life. I should've been dancing all the way home. When I received my trophy for the second high game, everyone cheered. I was not the best bowler in the league, but I came close one game.

For about one and a third seconds, I thought I might be a champion. That's how long it took me to realize that the true champion was sitting behind me. I wanted to be a champion, but I was not.

I was playing well. My friends were cheering me on. Even when I didn't get the high game, everybody was excited for me. Everybody except one. What happened to me?

I wasn't ready to be a champion because I was locked in an invisible dungeon. No one could see it, not even me.

What does it take to be a champion? You don't have to be the best. I wasn't even close to being the best bowler in the league.

You don't have to be the smartest. When I graduated from high school, I was not the valedictorian. I was in the National Honor Society. I received the award for the best math student and the award for the best science student. I was in the Top Ten in my class of about three hundred students.

The graduation was held indoors because there was a prediction for rain that evening. Each person walked to the platform to receive a diploma. When my name was announced, there was a clap of thunder and the lights blinked.

I wasn't the best academically.

I was a champion and didn't know it. I was looking at what I had *not* accomplished instead of the gifts that I clearly displayed. I was being prepared for a mission that only I could accomplish. I needed someone to unlock the door and set me free.

Alaska

Our neighborhood was next to the high school. Even though it was a short walk, I got cold in the winter if I didn't wear the proper clothes. Along with my winter coat, I had a hat with flaps that came down over my ears. I also wore gloves. I had poor blood circulation, so my hands, feet, and ears were cold easily.

When I arrived one chilly winter morning, the buses were unloading in front of the school. Most of the students wanted to be cool. They didn't care if they were cold. Wearing gloves was usually not necessary, but no one else wore a hat. That didn't bother me because I did not want to be cold.

There were a lot of problems in some high schools. The teachers at our school were required to sit in the hallway as the students were arriving. I didn't think that it was necessary.

Our school had several entrances in the front of the building. There was at least one teacher in each of the front hallways. When I walked in, I saw the teacher that was on duty. Everybody liked her. She was a good teacher and a lot of fun. She was a slow starter in the morning. She was sitting in a chair right outside of her room with a cup of coffee on a little table. She was looking at the morning newspaper, but her eyes were barely open.

I approached the teacher and greeted her in a friendly manner. She recognized my voice and didn't look up from the newspaper. She asked me why I arrived early. I told her that I wasn't that early. When she looked up from her newspaper, she said, "Rich?"

I answered, "Yes."

She said, "You look like it is Alaska out."

I said, "It feels like it is."

She always had something fun to say, so I waited.

She took a sip from her cup of coffee but did not say anything.

I said, "I am concerned that most of the high school students don't have winter clothes. They don't look any different today than they did two months ago."

She said, "I hope you have a good day."

I said, "I'll see you in English class."

Since there was no response, I walked toward my locker to get ready for my first class.

When I arrived in English class, the teacher didn't say anything about our conversation from the morning.

The teachers were concerned that the kids would get a copy of an exam so they could cheat. This was before everything was done on a computer. They had a mimeograph, which was a stencil machine combined with an ink roller. Rather than using an additive process to make the necessary pages, the mimeograph relied on a master page, often made of wax, that had elements stenciled out. The ink was then forced through the holes in the master page, producing high-quality copies.

For about an hour after the copies were made, there was an interesting smell.

The teachers were careful about how many copies of an exam they made. My English teacher took the copies and wrote a student's name at the top of each one. When it was time to take the exam, the teacher handed the personalized exam papers to the students.

Our school was built from six-sided modules called pods. They were placed next to each other in such a way that to stay in the front of the building, you had to alternate left and right turns. If you made two left turns in a row, you would find yourself at the back of the building instead of the front. Each pod had a letter assigned to it. Each of the rooms within the pod had a number that started with its letter. For new students, it was not easy to find a classroom.

My brother was two years older than me. He gave me advance instructions about the school. As I was graduating eighth grade, I wondered if I would find my way into the high school building. The layout of the rooms was just part of the mystery. The school was created as an experiment. Some of the things were found to be unmanageable and we're being phased out. Even the students who were already in high school were confused at the beginning of each new school year.

When I was a junior, there was a rumor floating around that the new male-female policies were going to make their way into the physical education program. There were concerns that the girls were not given the same opportunities that the boys were.

There were a lot of things that affected me during my high school years. Surface things like students making fun of me because of the clothes I wore were easily tolerated. Certain ideologies that crept into the school system from our society created great concerns for me. I struggled with how to deal with them.

Castles in the Sand

One of the things I dearly miss is peaceful times with special friends. I still have friends—special friends—but things just aren't the same.

I still recall the times that I spent lying on the sand on the edge of a pond. Mike and Laura's kids were still young. I teased them as they ran back and forth between where we were to the edge of the water. Mike and Laura baked in the sun half asleep while I watched the kids to make sure they didn't drown.

David's favorite pastime was to bury someone in the sand. Of course, I allowed him to bury me instead of his dad. It was more fun because I wiggled my way out of the sand when I was about half covered. David laughed and told me to wait until I was completely covered. I wasn't that fond of sand to be buried in it alive.

Cheri's idea of fun was to go to the edge of the water, bring back a bucket of water, and dump it on someone. The bucket wasn't big, but it was a surprise to her mom or dad to be woken up by a splash of cold water on their sunburned bodies.

When the kids were tired of their playful antics, we built sandcastles. David loved to mold the buildings out of the sand bucket. Cheri liked to push the sand up into a hill and dig into it to make the rooms.

Our bliss was always followed by a severe case of sunburn no matter how carefully we put on suntan lotion. All the splashing around managed to let some sun on our fair skin. I was told that getting sunburned meant that you had a good time. I must not have had good times.

There is much to be said for the tranquil life, but kids grow up. I still dwell on those times and the memories they hold. I no longer have time to build castles in the sand.

CHAPTER 6

Growing Up

Endurance

You never know what your body will do until you put it to the test. I was usually careful to not get myself into difficult situations. But when it happened, I was not good at getting myself out.

I led a protective life. I rarely did physically straining jobs. I managed to avoid them.

I had my share of tough spots to get out of, but they were always mind-bending.

I recall an experience when I had to go for an extended period with virtually no relief. It was an experience that I've tried to block out of my mind.

It was a cool summer morning in July when I arrived at the Christian bookstore. I was offered a job to go to Atlantic City to help load some materials that the owner purchased at a convention.

I arrived at the store at 9:00 a.m. and was promptly greeted by one of my friends who was offered the same job. It seemed like an enjoyable experience being able to work with David, a close friend that I had known for several years.

Then came the dilemma. The two regular employees who were planning to go had no idea that both of us were asked to go with them. The truck they had rented had a large front seat but not large enough for the four of us.

After some "no, you go" type of polite expressions between David and me, I finally agreed to go, and David agreed to forgo this opportunity. Little did he know that he got the best end of the deal.

Riding in a truck for a couple of hours was not my idea of fun, even though I managed to get a feeling of excitement. I was on a fascinating adventure and I was getting paid. Little did I know how little I would get for the effort.

Around noon, we arrived in Atlantic City. The city isn't as glamorous as people make it out to be. It is another city with bad traffic and not-so-friendly drivers.

The area around the convention center was not designed for the number of trucks that typically end up there at one time. The alleys are short and narrow, and it is difficult to see the one-way signs due to the trucks parked along the side of the street.

We turned onto a narrow street lined with trucks. We met a car going the wrong way on a one-way street. There was not enough room for us both. As we attempted to squeeze by the car, the latch on the side of our truck caught on a truck parked on our side.

We determined that our truck now had a door that would not latch properly, but there was no damage to the other truck. The car breaking the law went untouched.

After what seemed like an endless wait, a policeman finally showed up and took down the incident report.

I excused myself to hunt down a restroom. When I got back, I was told that I was voted to stay with the truck while the two other guys hunted for the boss. They said that they would be back soon.

Many people spend hours without eating, drinking, or resting. They have conditioned their bodies to take all kinds of abuse. If I didn't eat for a couple of hours, I started planning for the next opportunity to do so.

I had not eaten anything since breakfast. Hours passed and still no news from the happy adventurers.

Atlantic City, New Jersey, in July, is supposed to be fun if you are on the beach or losing your money, but sitting in a big old truck in the sun with no food or drink was no fun.

Around 6:00 p.m., things started to happen. My buddies came back with the word that our number had finally come up and we could back our truck to the loading dock.

Loading on an empty stomach was difficult, but I survived.

Two more hours of riding in the truck and we arrived at the store. We unpacked the stuff and went to eat together before returning home.

As I returned home with my $25 paycheck and a full stomach, I quickly forgot the fact that I had endured a typical day.

Midnight Mechanic

I am a morning person. Ever since I can remember, I preferred to go to bed early and wake up early. The sun often wakes me on Saturday mornings, the only day I can sleep in. I look at the clock and try to hide my face so I can go back to sleep.

When I was still living with my parents, I frequently had friends at our house. We rotated the location for Bible studies, and there was always a reason to just get together.

On one occasion, I can vividly recall the events that led to a most unusual climax for a seemingly usual singles' meeting at my house.

On this night, Nancy's radiator sprang a leak. She managed to get her car almost to my house. She showed up late with an interesting story.

After the meeting was over, a few of the guys pushed Nancy's car up the street so that it found a home right in front of my house. Being a late hour on Saturday night, Nancy left the car and got a ride home with a friend.

Nancy's brother-in-law is a mechanic. Skip came over the next afternoon to check out the damage.

Nancy and most of her relatives, including Skip, lived in Pennsylvania, about thirty miles away. After Skip considered the damage, he retired for the day and made plans to bring his tools the next evening.

Skip was working evenings at a shop close to my house, which was convenient for him to stop by on his way home. I asked Skip what time he expected to arrive on Monday night. He said to expect him around 10:00 p.m., which seemed OK to me and my family.

Car repairs are a tricky business, and few people can predict how long a job will take. Sure enough, Skip was late arriving Monday night. We weren't sure when he arrived since we had all gone to bed.

I am a light sleeper. When I woke in the middle of the night, I heard an unusual sound outside the front window. I noticed two police cars in the street and a light under the hood of Nancy's car. Sleepy eyes and pajamas accompanied me as I quietly went out the front door.

I asked one of the police officers, "Is there a problem here, officer?"

He responded, "Not if this man is supposed to be working on this car."

The cool night filled my sleepy lungs. A man emerged from the front seat of the disabled car.

"Skip?" I asked in a sheepish voice.

I still do not know Skip's real name. Apparently, the police officers didn't seem to care since they took my casual address as being a sign of friendship.

Fighting off a yawn, I spoke frankly, "This car belongs to his sister-in-law."

Skip was happy to see a familiar face.

I went back to bed, but not to sleep. I had a problem falling asleep, wondering if Skip was going to finish the job before someone else caused him any more difficulties.

The Lord has His hand on all of us. However, I never expected that my light sleeping was going to give me an opportunity to save a mechanic and address a police officer, all while in my pajamas.

A Little Bit of Life

Just before I graduated high school, my father encouraged me to start looking for a part-time job that could help me learn what it was going to be like to earn a living. I had some odd jobs here and there—cutting lawns, babysitting, tutoring, and inventory for retail stores—but I did not have a job that was steady and presented me with the challenge of responsibility.

My first regular job was at a local convenience store. It was close by, and I felt comfortable working there because the area was known for its friendly atmosphere and low crime rate.

I was hired by an enterprising young man who took the store and made some orders of it. He had only been the manager of the store for about two weeks when he hired me. About half of the items in the store were not marked with a price, and I had a hard time figuring out the prices from the price book.

The sodas, bread, and dairy products were marked on the shelves, so I could get those prices easily. Fortunately, around 90 percent of all that was sold in the store fit into those categories. The candy and cigarettes were also quite easy to remember since there were only a few prices.

The rest of the food in the store was a real mystery to me unless someone had priced the individual items. I got a break since I usually worked on the weekends. The grocery delivery was supposed to come on Friday morning. If it didn't come until late on Friday, I did the pricing myself. That helped me remember.

To comply with a town ordinance, the store had to close by 10:00 p.m. I liked that. I was the only employee in the store when I worked in the evenings. That was frightening at first, but I got used to the fact that there weren't any customers who came into the store to shoplift. If I were in the dairy refrigerator when someone came in, I hurried back to the counter. The customers waited for me.

There were a few customers who didn't like my adherence to the rules. I locked the door at 10:00 p.m. One night when the clock said 10:05 p.m., a customer knocked on the door and pleaded for me to let her in. I followed the rules and said, "Sorry, past 10:00 p.m. I am closed."

The woman called the next day and lied about the time because she was upset. She said that it was 9:40 p.m. and I locked up early. The manager told me that he had to write up the complaint even though he believed me. That was a rule, and he followed the rules too.

Overall, I enjoyed my experience at the store. The employees were nice to work with and I learned a lot.

During the year and a half that I worked at the store, there were four managers. My dad said that he wasn't surprised. When managers were good, they got a better store quickly. When there is trouble, the organization finds a way to cut down on tensions.

I thought that I did well considering it was my first responsible job. However, my competence got me in trouble with one manager. She was concerned that I was trying to take her job.

One Friday evening before she left, she told me that she quit because of a disagreement between her and the area supervisor. I was not worried. That weekend, the rest of the employees wanted to rearrange the work schedule for the next week. I agreed to rework the schedule and got the concurrence of all involved.

When I came into work Monday evening, our manager was back. She was upset because I was involved with changing the work schedule.

On another occasion, she called me at the store and fired me because I would not work on a Sunday morning. The person scheduled to work that Sunday morning got sick Friday night.

I asked to have Sunday mornings off for religious reasons. The manager agreed to this request upfront when she started at the store. She fired me anyway. I asked if I should lock the store and go home right away. She said that I could finish the evening shift. About an hour later, she called and rehired me.

I finally gave up that job because it was too taxing on my time and my emotions. I was still at the University of Delaware.

About the time I gave up that job, I found an interesting

29

programming job on the university campus. Taking a part-time job at the university was a good career move since I ended up with a professional position there after graduation. Some locks are easily unlocked. Others are more of a challenge.

PART II

The University

CHAPTER 7

Advanced Learning

Poetry Class

I always loved poetry. Most of my early poems had a similar pattern and rhyming scheme. Each stanza was usually four lines with alternating lines rhyming. As I developed my skills and wanted to put more of my emotion in my poems, a few of them became lengthy.

When I was at the University of Delaware, I took two poetry classes. The first one was reading poems and the second one was writing poems. I didn't like the reading poems class, but it introduced me to many different styles of poetry. When I started experimenting, some of my poems didn't turn out the way I expected.

When I took the writing class, I wondered how to receive a good grade. When the teacher explained what was expected in the class and how he was going to grade, I was no longer concerned. I was confused. The grading was going to be subjective. I should not have been surprised. How can anyone say whether a poem is good or not?

If a student turned in all the assignments, the grade was guaranteed to be a C. To obtain a B, the student's poems would need to have some freshness. I had no idea what that meant. I didn't ask the teacher.

The teacher reserved the As for students he recommended for the writer's workshop. I assumed that meant that the student was a serious poet. I was not and I wasn't planning to be one. I loved poetry and I took the class for my degree.

The poetry teacher was a short soft-spoken man. It was difficult for me to tell how old he was. He had an unkempt beard and he probably never combed his hair. He carried a satchel over his shoulder. When I described the teacher to my dad, he said, "That is exactly what I expected him to look like."

During the first session, the teacher showed the students a notebook that he recommended. It was a bound book that was 8.5 by 11 inches and about two inches thick. All the pages were blank and had no lines. It reminded me of a book that an artist might use for rough sketches. He said that when you are creating a poem, you should not be restricted by lines or borders. He indicated that creating a poem was like creating a drawing.

The teacher said that a poem reflects your life. He said something like this: "The poem you write today is affected by everything you have seen, heard, experienced, and thought up to the time that you wrote the poem." I concluded that it was virtually impossible to recreate a poem that you had forgotten. When you write the poem the second time, there are additional things in your life that are going to affect how you write the poem.

There are many things about this professor that seemed unusual to me; however, most of what he said sounded wise. I did not disagree with anything he said. He had an unusual outlook on life, but it was intriguing.

As I considered his statement about trying to recreate a poem, I was beginning to understand how the things that happened when I was young are now influencing the way I think about my life.

I started to ask myself questions like "Did certain things that happened to me when I was young permanently define who I would ultimately become?" If it were possible to be unlocked, how would I do that? Would I be able to help others who have been locked up?

By the end of the class, I decided that I liked it. I don't think I would've taken another class by this professor, but it was enjoyable as well as educational. I finished all the assignments, so I was sure that

I was going to get a C in the class. I still couldn't figure out what freshness was and I did not care.

When I received my grade for the course, I was pleasantly surprised. The professor gave me a B.

Math Class

Math is your friend. Your budget is your friend. Calculus is your friend.

I repeated those phrases many times to my friends and those that I was tutoring. Some people thought I was being funny.

It is not a joke. I believe that math is crucial for understanding many things in life. Calculus is not everyone's friend, but if you need it, it can be. The fundamentals of mathematics are the basis for so much in our society. That is why I wanted to be a math teacher. I didn't want anyone to be handicapped by not having a basic understanding of the principles of math.

When I was in high school, math classes were fun. There were other subjects that I did not enjoy when I was in school. There may be a place for me to discuss that, but not here.

Before attending university, I took an advanced placement test for calculus. I did well enough that I did not have to take the first of three semesters of calculus at the University of Delaware. My high school calculus class prepared me to enter directly into the second semester of calculus.

The first session of my first class of calculus started at 8:00 a.m. on Monday. Because I can say this with certainty, do not think that I have an incredible memory. There is something about this class that allowed the memory to stay in a special compartment in my brain. I don't know what the name of that compartment is, but when something gets in, it is always immediately available.

Most of the students in this class were like me. It was the first class after summer break and it was early in the morning. The students must've been desperate to take this class.

I don't like things to distract me. When I go into a large room, I try to sit in a seat with minimal distractions. There was a seat in the front row on the left side of the auditorium.

The professor for this class was Oriental. My experience with Orientals has been good. I respect their desire to excel in academics. Most are polite and soft-spoken. They're able to get things done but in an efficient and kind way. I had no reason to believe that this professor would be any different.

Within a short period, I recognized that this professor did not like to just lecture. He wanted the class to be engaged. I had no objection to that. It was unusual, but still a style that I respected.

Since the professor did not know the names of the students, when he wanted someone to answer a question, he had a strategy. First, he asked for a volunteer. If no one volunteered, he selected someone by their shirt color or row number. He also pointed to a person close to where he was standing.

As the class proceeded, fewer people were able to correctly answer his questions. Most of the students were not ready for the first class. Who spends time reviewing what was learned in the previous semester?

The teacher asked the question, "What is the fundamental theorem of calculus?" It was familiar to me, but I had not memorized it.

No one raised their hand. When a student did not answer a question correctly, the teacher said something that dishonored the person. The students did not want to be put down, so they stopped volunteering.

The teacher was standing close to me when he asked this question. The teacher pointed to me. I had about two seconds to decide what I was going to say. My answer was, "I don't remember." That was the truth. I did not remember.

The teacher snickered and looked around the room for someone else to answer the question. I was amazed that a student raised his hand. The teacher called on the student, and he answered the question in an acceptable way. The teacher praised the student.

Meanwhile, I was wondering whether I should continue to sit in my seat or leave. I decided to stay.

Near the end of the session, the professor came near me again. He stopped as if he were thinking. I could tell he was a good teacher. I just didn't like the way he responded to students who didn't know the answers. I was OK because I didn't answer the question.

I thought the professor would keep pacing, but he didn't. He continued to stand about six feet in front of me. He looked at me and said, "I have been thinking about the answer that you gave earlier in the class."

I wondered if we were in the same classroom. I did not answer the question. I said I did not know the answer to the question.

The professor said, "How could you say that you do not remember what the fundamental theorem of calculus is? It is so important that no one should ever forget it."

I could say that I was shocked, but I wasn't. I was angry. Why would a teacher spend half of a class rehearsing in his mind how he was going to offend me?

I said nothing. The teacher walked away from me and finished the class.

I refused to be intimidated by this professor, but I couldn't allow that to happen again. Every day, I did something I thought I would never have to do. I sat in the middle of a row and the middle of the auditorium. I was careful not to wear anything that would stand out enough for him to call on me.

This wasn't the first time that something like this happened to me. I knew that I was easily embarrassed. My pride was getting in the way. I thought I was smart enough to not be intimidated by a university professor. He practiced so long that he was good enough to get away with something like this.

Where does that leave me? The professor only hurt me because I allowed him to. I learned from this experience.

Business Class

My academic advisor encouraged me to organize my classes so that I would earn a minor in business administration. The courses associated with this minor introduced me to things of the business world. Often, technical people know nothing about the business side of the company. The courses included business, economics, and accounting. A course in logic was also required, but I was already scheduled to take one for my computer science degree.

I was not able to find anything in my journals or notes that I saved from the university about business classes. However, I recall taking a course that required the students to be organized in teams to compete against each other.

I wondered how we would remember who was on our team. Athletic teams have different uniforms. I wondered if the teacher would give us a badge or something to hang around our neck to identify the teams, but nothing was provided.

One of the members of our team had toothpicks. I guess he had problems with food getting stuck in his teeth. I did, but I didn't carry toothpicks to school. Initially, it seemed to be insignificant, but later, I saw the benefit. The person with the toothpicks handed one to each member of his team. He didn't ask if we needed a toothpick for our teeth. He gave us one so that we would all have one in our mouth. We were the "toothpick team."

After we finished our project, the teacher asked us to identify things that we learned on the project that were significant. I said the toothpick generated team spirit. I don't know if the teacher acknowledged this or not. I believe it helped.

Computer Class

I survived my business classes. My computer classes were different. The first class I took was a basic programming course. There is not much to say about that class. The teacher taught us how to think like a computer. To demonstrate that we understood the basic principles, we were given a few computer programs to write. I liked this class and I did well. I learned what I needed to learn and I received an A.

When I was a junior, I took a course that taught the internal workings of the computer. Everything inside of a computer is a program. The main program keeps track of everything that's happening and who's doing it. This program is called the operating system. It is like a traffic cop.

The course required the students to understand the elementary parts of the operating system. In real life, it would take many experienced programmers several months or even years, working full-time, to write an operating system. Each team consisted of four students. We had approximately two months to write our operating system.

We were learning to work as a team. The team was going to be graded on the project. If one person knew what to do and was good at delegating, it would be easy to complete the project on time. The problem was that no one on our team was designated as the leader. That was trouble waiting to happen.

My team was able to organize our tasks. It seemed like each of the members had learned the principles. We were inexperienced programmers and we all had a different idea of how to put it all together.

The project appeared to be going well. Each person completed their tasks on time. As we were combining our modules, we identified problems. All the problems were related to miscommunications between the members. We did not have a clear direction for resolving the problems. We did not even know the extent of the problems.

Since there was no designated leader, the personalities of the members were significant. One of the members of my team assumed the role of leader by insisting that things be done his way. I was confident that we were not going to finish our project on time. I was sure that the program would not run. The only question was, "How would the instructor grade our program?"

There were five teams. One team successfully wrote an operating system. That team received an A. The other four teams presented their operating system which was nonfunctional. They received a B. I was grateful for a B.

While I was at the university, there were other classes that I had similar experiences in. It seemed like most of the technical courses were like that. My brother told me about the engineering courses that he took. Once he scored forty-five on an exam. He said that was a C. I asked him if that meant that about half of the bridges that were built probably would fall.

He told me that scoring exams at the university could not correlate with technical skills in real life.

CHAPTER 8

Application

Who's in Charge?

While I was working in the grocery store, I learned a lot of important things about life. One was, "Who's in charge?"

When I was working in the grocery store, the line of authority was clear to me. Someone owned the company. Someone oversaw a group of stores in a certain area. Someone oversaw the grocery store where I worked. It was delegated authority.

As a part-time employee, I had little responsibility and little authority. I was told what to do, when to do it, and how to do it. When something arose that required clarity, I checked with my manager. If the decision was wrong, I was not responsible. I was not ready for much responsibility or authority.

I continued to work at the grocery store during my first year at the university. My expenses were minimal because I was still living at home. The part-time job was sufficient. While I was a freshman at the university, I started thinking about my career. I was hoping to find an opportunity to gain experience in the computer field before I graduated.

There were several buildings at the university that had terminals connected to the large mainframe computers. The main computer building housed most of the computers and many computer terminals. It was a busy place during the day. By 9:00 p.m., things calmed down.

The students majoring in computer science had access to private rooms in the building that contained computer terminals and printers. I took advantage of those hideaways from time to time; however, I was in the main terminal room most of the time.

One day, I saw an advertisement for a part-time job. It said, "Become a PLATO programmer. Qualify for summer jobs." I had no idea what a PLATO programmer was, but it sounded interesting to me. I knew that I was going to have to step out and look for opportunities. Since the advertisement was on the wall in the main computer building, I assumed that the jobs would be on the university campus. I liked the idea of learning something new and getting paid to do it at the same time.

When I applied for the job, I was directed to attend training sessions. This was the only place I was going to learn to become a PLATO programmer. I liked the instructor and learning the programming language was easy for me. The programming language was designed for nonprogrammers. The focus was on designing an educational curriculum. I was excited that I was learning to use computers in education.

The instructor asked me if I had an area of interest. I told him that I was interested in mathematics. My first assignment was working with a math professor to help develop a curriculum for entry-level math students. It was a major win for me.

The PLATO system included specially designed computer terminals. The PLATO terminals were grouped to create a PLATO classroom. Some of the programmers were assigned to oversee a classroom. I was assigned to the classroom where the math students worked. I liked the idea of having most of my classes and my work location in the same building.

As soon as I realized that I could make enough money in this new job all year round, I resigned from my position at the grocery store.

I was assigned times in the computer classroom when the math students were there. Some of the professors had a few students using their programs. The math professor was engaging most of his students to use the classroom. Several times a day, the classroom was filled with math students.

The PLATO classrooms were scheduled so that drop-in students could usually find a terminal in some classrooms. My professor scheduled the whole classroom for his students. Some who worked for the PLATO organization were not aware of the need for the classroom to be exclusive for the math students.

One day when I was waiting for the math students to arrive, I thought of an easy way to notify the students who were still in the classroom. If there were just one or two, I probably would have quietly asked them to leave. On this day, the classroom was full of students who would have to leave in a few minutes.

As a moderator of the classroom, I was given permission to send a message to all the terminals in that classroom. My message was something like this: "In five minutes, this classroom will be reserved for math students. If you are not a math student, then you will have to leave. I'm sorry for the inconvenience."

As the students started to leave, one of the PLATO administrators approached me. She asked me why I was requiring all the students to leave the classroom. I told her that the classroom was reserved for the math students for the next hour.

It was obvious from the tone of her voice that she did not appreciate what I had done. She said, "How many math students? Hundreds of thousands?"

I wanted to be respectful to my superior. I said, "A math professor requested that this classroom be reserved for his students during certain hours. The scheduling staff approved his request. I could not think of a better way to inform all these students to leave in a few minutes. How should I do it next time?"

I could tell that the administrator did not like the decision to have a classroom completely reserved by one teacher. That was not my battle. As the classroom coordinator, I was given the responsibility and the authority to enforce the use of the classroom.

I'm glad that I had an opportunity to learn about authority early. It wasn't easy, but I was glad that I did. There were many times that

I had to deal with authority from both ends. If you don't get this right, you can feel like you are in bondage.

Dear Mr. Payne

Shortly before I graduated from the university with my bachelor's degree, the math professor that I was working with asked me if I would join him in his research. He received a grant from the National Science Foundation to develop a computer program that diagnosed errors that students were making in math. It was exciting and exactly what I was looking for, so I accepted his offer to work for him while I was taking courses toward my master's degree.

The professor was given space in the basement of an old building. There were three rooms. One room was the office where the professor, his secretary, and I had desks. The second room was a PLATO classroom dedicated to his math students. A third room was used for storage.

In addition to helping to develop and write the program, I was given the assignment to oversee the PLATO classroom.

There is nothing that lifts my spirits more than to read letters, cards, thank-you notes, and little trinkets.

I forgot much of what I had until I decided to write this book. I felt dry for material, so I pulled out my drawer full of days gone past.

The thing that struck me the hardest emotionally was the personal letters that my closest friends, mostly female, had written to me. I could almost hear their voices and see the emotion on their faces as I read words that were written many years before.

One might think that my ego was boosted by all the wonderful things that I read about myself, but quite the opposite. Emotions of yesteryear were resurrected as I read letters that I have no remembrance of. I remember the person and the fact that I received letters and cards, but the content sometimes took me by surprise.

I recall some of the things that people wrote to me, but most are like I received them in today's mail. Perhaps I am doing myself, and the senders, an injustice by keeping them in attempting to relive the days and emotions gone past.

The one thing, or more correctly things, that I always remember is the package of thank-you letters that Pam's class sent to me after they were my guests at the computer classroom at the University of Delaware.

I still recall as vividly as I recall anything the emotions I felt when I first read the letters from those grade school kids. Most of them were poorly written, but the fact that I knew these kids personally meant something special to me.

One boy came to me in the classroom and said, "Mr. Payne, don't let anyone use my computer while I go to the bathroom." A girl asked me why her keyboard had black and white keys instead of yellow and blue keys like everyone else's.

These seem to be trivial, if not uninteresting, but I was able to help them in their quest to learn more about the world they live in. That made my life a little sweeter and worth living.

I was just getting old enough to be called Mr. Payne by the children, so the sound of it was still intriguing and touched my emotions every time I heard it. When I opened the package from Pam's students, I was entering the life of adulthood. These third and fourth graders were the first to write me a letter that started, "Dear Mr. Payne".

The sound of it still does something to me, especially when people older than me address me that way. Sometimes it is just in jest, but often, it is a sign of respect, often where respect is somewhat lacking in general. To have earned such respect from children is one thing, but to receive it from the older generation is something to cherish.

The Wizard of UD

I was always hard on myself, harder than anyone else. Like most perfectionists, I always saw something that needed to be done better, some job that wasn't complete, or a task that wasn't done well enough. At times, it worked to my benefit, at times, to my undoing.

The university was a good place to learn to excel. Unlike high school, it was not possible to be the best at anything. There was always someone better, smarter, quicker, and studied harder. The grades often moved along with the abilities of the students, so to excel, you had to be better than all the rest, not just exceptional by your standards.

My desire to excel in everything overflowed into my work environment while at the university. I was excellent at all that I did according to my supervisors and barely acceptable according to me.

The secretaries often wondered what I did all day long. They never saw me, except when I stopped to chat. After a few moments, they would ask me what I was up to. I spent a good deal of my time simply waiting for a process to be completed on my computer, so it didn't appear to be time well spent both for them and for me. What is a person to do when technology has not progressed to the point of keeping up with requests?

The students were in awe of me because I fixed anything that went wrong. I could fix the terminals, the programs, and occasionally the temperature of the room. When all else failed, they called me. I came through with flying colors. There were some things that were beyond my abilities, but I got the job done even if it meant getting someone else to help.

The teaching assistants (TAs) were fun to be around. Some knew technology, but some did not. They were dedicated to helping their students learn.

I was the primary author of all the programs. Material came from the professors, but the workings were my handiwork. It was no wonder that I had all the answers. I created the access codes. The TAs wanted more abilities to access special features of the programs. I decided who got what, so they were nice to me. I didn't play favorites, but they didn't know that.

I greatly enjoyed this job at the university as well as the educational experience. I learned a great deal about computer technology, but even more about human interactions.

Courage

At the University of Delaware, the Memorial Hall was built in 1924 as the college library and a memorial to soldiers from Delaware killed during World War I. The PLATO classroom reserved for math students was originally in the basement. There were no windows and the air was always stale. I was glad that I could move around. I had a hard time sitting at my desk the whole day.

Sometimes, I worked at one of the terminals in the classroom when the classroom was empty. The terminal on my desk was connected to the same computer that the classroom terminals were connected to. When the secretary needed to talk to me, she walked across the hall. She didn't like being away from her desk because someone was always getting upset with her if she didn't answer the phone. We put a phone in the classroom so that it could be answered when the secretary was away from her desk.

The hallways were narrow. The Coke machine down the hall was always malfunctioning. Sometimes I put coins in the machine but I did not get a drink. Sometimes I saw coins sitting in the return slot. The coins fell when no one was there. A few times I saw a student hit the side of the machine. Several coins dropped into the coin return slot or a drink fell. More than once, I walked up to the machine and a can was sitting there waiting for me. I got a free Coke.

The restrooms on the ground floor were not maintained well. Some students were messy. We didn't know when the cleanup crew would come. After a while, they put a lock on the men's room door and gave the employees a key. After that, the restroom was acceptable.

One sunny morning during the summer, I realized that the humidity in the classroom was higher than it normally was. I asked the secretary to call someone to check the air-conditioning. A couple of hours passed and no one showed up. The humidity was almost unbearable. I was concerned that the high humidity was going to damage the terminals. I called the PLATO maintenance staff. They sent someone to assist me.

The PLATO terminals were expensive. They were designed for

educational purposes. Each terminal cost about $10,000. That was a lot of money back then. There were concerns that someone would steal the terminals out of the classroom, so they locked the terminals to the tables. We did not have keys to the terminal locks. The keys were held by the PLATO maintenance team.

When the lady showed up to assist me, she said that we would have to move the terminals to another room. We weren't sure where to move the terminals because we didn't know the source of the problem.

There was no master key for the locks that we used to secure the computer terminals. The maintenance lady started unlocking the locks with her large ring of keys. It would not have been a problem if she only needed to unlock one, but there were twenty terminals in the classroom. The locks and keys were not labeled, so it was a guessing game to find the right key.

After three or four of the terminals were unlocked, it became obvious that the source of the problem was directly behind the classroom. There were water pipes on the other side of the wall. Steam was coming through the wall and the ceiling. We went into the room next door, which was our storage room. The humidity was normal there, so I started moving the terminals.

The terminals were heavy. The top of a terminal could be disconnected from its base. I had the task of disconnecting the top part of each computer from its base and moving each piece into the room next door. Each piece was about fifty or sixty pounds.

Before I finished, it looked like a cloud was coming from the ceiling.

There was no one to help me move the terminals. I had to move all forty pieces by myself. It wasn't a long distance, but it was extremely difficult to do while breathing humid air.

After I successfully moved all the computer terminals to the storage room, a building maintenance person came and cut a hole in the wall where the steam was coming through. It was several days before we could use the classroom.

After this incident, the math professor realized that he needed to find another place for the PLATO classroom. We were happy with our new location. We had two large rooms in one of the newer buildings, still on the main campus. The students told me that they enjoyed the new location as well.

PART III

Single Life

CHAPTER 9

Why Me?

"In the year that King Uzziah died, I saw the Lord sitting upon a throne, high and lifted up; and the train of his robe filled the temple … And I heard the voice of the Lord saying, "Whom shall I send, and who will go for us?" Then I said, "Here I am! Send me" (Isaiah 6:1 and 6:8 ESV).

Yes, I am a Christian. Yes, I read the Bible. Yes, I believe that God speaks to His people. But you don't need to be a Christian to benefit from experiences in your life. Many of the people that I reference in this book were not Christians at the time. They may not be Christians now. However, I am grateful for all that I've learned from them. I can learn from anyone, even if the person is different from me.

There were moments in my life when things changed dramatically. Some were easy to identify, like graduating from high school and graduating from the university. Most people can identify with these life-changing events. For some, the changes are for the good. It is an opportunity to mature. It is an opportunity to set a direction for your life. It is an opportunity to leave difficult things behind and believe in a brighter future. It is a time to rejoice.

Tragically, there are examples of increased difficulty associated with these life-changing moments.

One of the hardest things for me was when my growth was

interrupted too soon. I say too soon because I know there will always be interruptions during the greatest times of growth. I want some time for my new growth to become obvious to myself and those around me before a storm threatens to destroy all my gains.

A few months before I graduated high school, I started working in a small grocery store close to my house. I liked the manager. He was young, full of energy, and hope. He encouraged me to persevere through those first few weeks as we dug through the chaos that a previous manager left to him. It looked promising for our little inexperienced team.

I continued to work at this store when I started attending the University of Delaware. I lived at home so that I could save money. It was a short distance from my house to the university. It was a short distance from my house to the grocery store. However, there was still a lot of coming and going. It wasn't the best scenario, but a good start.

My mom had cancer. My brother was still at the university. My dad had a full-time job. My sister was still a young teenager who could not drive. It was an exciting time, but a difficult time for our family. My mom died during my first summer at the university.

After four years at the university and receiving my bachelor's degree, I continued to go to school part-time while I worked at the university. After another four years, I changed directions in my career. It was 1985. The economy in our country was not going well. I wanted a different kind of job but still with computers. I looked for a job in the Wilmington area, but I was not successful. My dad and several of my friends were helping me. But even with their support and referrals, I did not get hired by DuPont or the other places I applied to.

I enjoyed where I lived. I enjoyed my church. I enjoyed my friends. I enjoyed life in the Wilmington area. It was quiet, slow, and less threatening than many of the areas that I heard about in the rest of the country. I did not want to leave Wilmington. It seemed like an exciting time of my life, but I was unaware of the storm that was coming. It was a different kind of storm than I ever experienced.

When I graduated high school, the career counselors were helpful

REMOVE THE LOCK 🔒

at my school. They told me to never burn any bridges. They said that if I applied for a job but took a different job, I needed to consider the possibility of working for that company sometime in the future. That advice came through for me.

When I graduated from college, I applied for a job with IBM in Gaithersburg, Maryland. They offered me a job, but I turned it down because I decided to stay at the university and continue with my master's degree. When I was looking for another job, I went back to IBM in Gaithersburg, Maryland, and asked them if they would consider me. They said that they had no open positions at their facility; however, there were openings in Bethesda, Maryland. Bethesda is not far from Gaithersburg. I accepted a job with IBM in Bethesda.

When I left home for the first time, it seemed like a good opportunity for me to grow. I was not cutting off everyone from my past, but I was physically far away from them. They were no longer a regular influence in my life.

My dad helped me find a nice apartment that was within a few miles of my work location. In some ways, it reminded me of home. Even though I was just a mile away from a metro station and a busy highway, when I was in my apartment, I felt like it was a retreat center. The area was shaded, and I lived at the end of a dead-end street. It was quiet, and mothers were not afraid to walk with their small children.

For the first few months, I often visited my family and friends on weekends. I was lonely. I was afraid. I was hesitant to take the big steps that I needed to take.

I hate traffic. Most people do, but I really hate traffic. The traffic in North Bethesda was more than I had ever experienced. Even though I was a few miles away from my work location, it took me about twenty minutes to get home. I didn't want to go anywhere in the evenings or on Saturdays. There was no rush hour where I lived. The traffic was bad all the time, even in the middle of the night.

The apartment that I was renting was expensive. I could afford it because I had a well-paying job. I found a grocery store that was within a few miles of my house. It wasn't the grocery store that I was used to, but I found what I needed. I found a place to dry-clean my suits. I wore a suit at IBM. The suit had to be expensive, and my shoes were expensive. The taxes were high. People were not friendly when I walked out of my neighborhood or into the stores.

It was a good life. I was happy some of the time, but more often, I was thinking about home. Why did I have to leave? What was I supposed to be doing? Was I no longer the person I wanted to be? Would I ever be in a place where I could use the things that I learned to help people? How was I supposed to help people if I didn't know anyone who wanted help?

IBM was a fun company to work for. I liked my coworkers. I liked some of my managers. I liked what I was doing. I was good at what I was doing, and most people knew it. I felt good about my job.

Many of my coworkers were familiar with the local restaurants. Someone suggested going out to lunch. I thought about it too much, but then I stopped thinking about it. I went with them whether I knew where they were going or not. I was sure I could find something on the menu that I liked. We went to restaurants that I would never have considered going to. I was hungry and wanted to have lunch. My coworkers understood and said that they would help me find something on the menu that I would enjoy. They always did. They liked me and wanted me to have fun times with them.

One of my coworkers was a young Oriental lady. When she got married, she invited her coworkers to her wedding and the reception. That was a new experience for me. I liked the young lady, and I wanted to be there on her joyous day.

Many days, I woke up and cried. I asked myself, "What did I do? Why am I here? I feel like I'm in prison. What can I do to become free? Who will help me? Who can I trust?"

When I am deep in thought or overcome by a strong emotion, I write a poem. It is a way for me to release something. After I wrote the poem, I read it like someone gave it to me. It encourages me to read my poem. I feel blessed that someone gave the poem to me during my difficult time. I wonder if I can share this wonderful gift

56

with somebody else who is struggling in a similar way. Perhaps this is part of the answer I am looking for.

Acrostic Despair
01/02/88

Alone in the desert of time
Sits a man of lonely despair
Recording the moment in rhyme
Wondering if there's one to care.

Between thoughts of glimmering hope
And the joy of happier days
Lies the moments in which to cope
And the passions of classic plays.

Carefully, thoughts are written down
And emotions are captured then
As he gazes at the town
And back to his paper again.

Deep from within his caring heart
Comes a sign of great compassion
As he waits for the mood to start
And ignores the present fashion.

Even if no one hears his thought
He speaks it nonetheless today;
Even if it may be for naught
There's a message for it to say.

CHAPTER 10

The Real Me

Hidden Blessings

What Did You Do This Summer?

I like to think that a day does not go by that I am not given the opportunity to witness someone in some way. Summers can go by so fast that you wonder what you did for the last three months.

For some, summer is synonymous with the beach. For me, summer is synonymous with moving. People seem to love to move during the summer.

I used to think that moving was just another one of those things that life threw at you occasionally. All my past experiences with moving people have been chores. However, this summer was different.

I moved to a new apartment last June. Fully expecting this to be a real chore, I reluctantly asked assistance from some of my friends at Bible study. All I needed were a few able bodies to help me move my furniture. I wasn't ready to be blessed by the Lord, nor was I expecting this to be a time to witness.

On the day of the move, it rained and rained and rained. I knew that the Lord was with me in this move, so I asked the Lord to hold back the rain while I moved. So that I would believe that my prayer was answered, the Lord stopped the rain only ten minutes before the appointed time to begin the move. Normally, this would have been just an answer to prayer, but that day, it was much more.

The number of people who showed up was overwhelming, and the way we worked together and enjoyed ourselves was an added blessing. Jim, my friend from work, was also there to help. Perhaps a seed was planted that day in Jim's heart. He had never experienced that kind of love. Later, he said to me, "I am happy for you. You really have some special friends."

As we finished packing the trucks and cars, Jim looked up at the dark clouds and said, "You better pray that it doesn't rain." I was surprised that he remembered how important prayer was to me.

In all sincerity, I replied, "I already prayed. That's why it stopped raining."

Not even a single drop of rain fell on us that evening. That was an answer to my prayer, but the Lord had a lot more to accomplish that evening. There was no out-of-pocket cost to me because one of my friends brought two of his trucks—that was blessing two. Jim experienced the love of the Lord—that was blessing three. Jim observed my answer to prayer—that was blessing four.

You're probably wondering why I shared this story with you. I wasn't sure myself. I wrote the story last Saturday, and I later realized that it didn't tell the whole story. I keep a diary. After rereading the story, I thought of going back to my diary to see what I had written two years ago.

After my first summer away from my family and friends in Wilmington, I wrote the following:

"There is a strangeness in my spirit. As the cool breezes of fall move in, I have a strange feeling of loneliness ... A season of quiet and loneliness ..."

Contrasting my feelings of 1985 with 1987, I realized that the difference was my friends. Even though I had been a Christian for almost twenty years, I was lonely without Christian friends to share my life with.

Tears came to my eyes as the words of Jim echoed in my mind: "You really have some special friends." Jim of 1987 is like Rich of

1985. Jim does not have Christ in his life. Even though the Holy Spirit lived in me, Christ was not real in my life. Without Christian friends to share the love of God, we can easily fall into a depression of loneliness.

By the time you read this article, Jim will be in Minnesota. While he was here, my friends and I were able to share some of God's love with him. For a little while, Jim was not so lonely. We can be sure that he will remember why.

Let us pray that we will not miss the opportunities to share God's love with the Jims of this world. That is why we are here.

As I considered the things that happened in my life that created a lock, I wondered if there was anything that unlocked a lock for me. When I read this entry, I realized that having true friends can significantly change your outlook on life.

My friend, Jim, seemed like someone that you would not be concerned for. He made friends easily and worked well with his teammates. After he moved, he invited me to visit his family in Minnesota. On the outside, it appeared that Jim had few cares in his life. But this story indicates that he wished he had friends like I did.

Mr. Parmesan

Just a short note about eating. Like most people, I enjoy doing it, but not nearly as much as the opportunities that eating together provides. Lunch, a coffee break, or a quick bite to eat are often reasons to get together—those times are priceless in developing relationships.

A quaint little restaurant after a Sunday evening church service was often the birthplace of many heart-to-heart talks between friends.

On one such occasion, I went along with about a dozen of my new single friends from church. It was around 9:00 p.m. and almost everyone wanted a dessert, a soda, or a cup of coffee. Not me! I was starving because I usually ate dinner after the church service on Sunday evenings.

We had a friendly waitress that evening. Everyone else ordered a bit of this or that. When she finally got to me, I ordered the veal Parmesan dinner. In her hometown, laughing way, she exclaimed, "Veal Parmesan? How did you get connected to this group?" Of course, everyone laughed, including me.

We had a great time together, sharing lightly and meaningfully with our friends. The waitress got involved and had a good time with us. Our lighthearted humor was also witnessed by her as we showed that a group of singles can have a good time and remain respectable.

Many times after that, the waitress addressed me with great respect as Mr. Parmesan. I represented the odd yet accepted minority in the family of God.

When I read this story about myself, I wondered how I survived. Why were they my friends? How long could they remain my friends? What was a true friend?

Would I remain true to myself? Having a different eating habit from my friends appeared to be insignificant. However, feeling like I was different from everyone else was a concern. Was I just uncomfortable or did this realization put me in an emotional prison?

Paper Airplanes

No matter how hard you try to deny it, there are times when you need to leave your stoic adult nature behind and allow yourself to enjoy life. I can never manage to do this by myself. I need a catalyst. My friends are my best agents—the younger, the better.

My friend, Andrew, just turned five. He's creative, attentive, and full of life. He never sits still and he plays until he drops. Occasionally, he frustrates his mother, but we all love him dearly. We wouldn't want him to change even one bit (well, maybe just one little bit).

Children are amazing. They never seem to run out of fun things to do. I love to play children's games. It clears my brain and calms my nerves. The simple essence of play disarms me. I'm able to release my inner desire to run, shout, and be carefree—the tension-release mechanism that we so carefully remove from every well-adjusted adult.

There are times to be serious. There are times to be calm and carefully execute life's plans. But to go continually in that mode, with no time to just be childlike and silly, greatly adds to the unreleased tensions that beset each one of us. If left unchecked, the state of tension-upon-tension and stress-upon-stress begins to pay its toll on even the best of us.

As I write this treatise on stress release, I am reminded of a recent episode with Andrew. While he was at my house, we entertained ourselves by making paper airplanes. Almost a week later, they are still sitting on my coffee table, virtually untouched from the moment Andrew left. I am usually prompt at cleaning my living room after guests leave, but not this time. I purposely left the paper airplanes to remind me of my fun time with my little friend. It was an inspiration to continue to write.

Just looking upon the tangible results of our fun time together recreates a little bit of excitement and releases some of the tension built up over the day.

For fear that others will not understand, I will now remove these relics before any uninitiated guests stop by unannounced.

My Name Ain't Mike

As time goes by, I am often amazed at how many different types of people there are in this world. There are psychologists who have attempted to classify people by their general personality traits, but even they agree that most people are a mixture of two or more of these traits in varying degrees.

Most of my friends say that I am primarily melancholic. My mood swings and analytical tendencies give me away. I am sure that I have a unique mix of all four temperaments, but everyone I ask gives me a slightly different answer to the question, "How much of the other temperaments do you think that I have?"

My analytical side does me as much harm as it does good. My friends say that I am too hard on myself. I like to analyze—and often overanalyze—common things. For example, what makes a person continually make the same mistake?

I'm not much for socializing, but I am working on that. I try hard to be friendly and pleasant to everyone that I meet, but it isn't natural for me, and it shows.

Each of my neighbors has their own way of being neighbors. Some wave when I go by, some say "hi" and some just smile. A few stop by to chat for a while when we see each other in the yard.

One of my neighbors continually calls me Mike. It took me a while to figure out why. There are two people who live close to me with the name Mike. He must've gotten me mixed up with one of the other two. He stops by often to use my phone or just say "hi," but he always calls me Mike. His wife and kids call me Mike too. That's no mystery. I told him several times what my name was, but he kept forgetting.

I finally decided to let him call me Mike. Mike is a nice name. I can think of lots of other names that I would like to be called less.

But my name ain't Mike!

I thought it was OK. I would let my neighbor call me Mike. Adults do things like that, but kids don't. When a child asks why something is unusual, ignoring the question isn't going to satisfy.

My heart has always been for children who have a rough life. There are many boys who need a father, an older brother, or a friend to help them learn how to grow up to be a man. I believed that was part of my purpose in life.

As well as enjoying little boy games, Andrew notices when something isn't quite right. Andrew visits me from time to time when his mom needs some time off.

When I can't think of something for Andrew to do, I suggest that he play outside with the neighborhood boys and girls. He likes the kids in my neighborhood. One day when Andrew was playing outside, I went to my mailbox.

As I approached, Andrew and one of the neighborhood boys were having a heated discussion. Andrew said, "Here he is now. We will ask him."

I said, "Ask me what?"

Andrew said, "He says your name is Mike. I told him he's wrong. Your name is Rich."

Andrew was talking to the son of my neighbor down the street who thinks my name is Mike. Now I was in trouble. What was I going to do?

The other boy said, "Your name is Mike, right?"

I said, "Different people call me different names. It's OK for you to call me Mike if you want to."

Andrew said, "But your name is Rich. I know it is. All your friends call you Rich."

I said, "It's OK, Andrew. You don't have to argue over my name. I think it's time for us to go to lunch. Are you hungry?"

Andrew said, "Sure, Mr. Rich. Let's go to lunch."

The other boy looked at me with a frown, but he didn't say anything.

I thought the discussion wasn't over with Andrew. I was surprised that he didn't bring it up again.

Charlotte's Farm

I receive great enjoyment from helping others. But that is not my primary motivation for service. God has called each one of us to serve. That is reason enough.

God is a considerate God. He has made us in such a way that we enjoy doing things for others. This is not the natural man, but rather the new, spiritual nature that God gives us when we accept His plan.

The farm has always been a place for family, friends, and neighbors to rally around. Trying to do big tasks by yourself is difficult, if not impossible. They can become enjoyable when many work together. With large tasks, the effort of many working together always surpasses the sum of each effort. There are some things that simply require more than one person.

Recently, seven of us went to help Charlotte fix up her

grandparents' farm. In one weekend, we were able to accomplish far more than Charlotte could ever have done by herself. Charlotte's two weekends per month were barely enough to do the routine upkeep. We were able to tackle many outside chores that have slowly become next to impossible.

The farm is also a place for reflection. It reminds me of the years gone past when life was much simpler and space was plentiful. We worked and joked around with hardly an interruption from the rest of the world. Our only visitors were people coming to view the house and the land that was just put on the market.

In the evening, we built a bonfire from the tree limbs and watched the sparks rise high above our heads into the vast reaches of the winter sky. As the time drew near to retire, Dave and I entertained everyone with our rendition of putting out the fire with only one bucket of water.

As the time for our departure drew near, we scurried to get one last thing done before we left. We didn't want to leave, but we all knew that the fast-paced world awaited our return. We knew that we would have other opportunities to serve one another, whether back at the farm or someplace else. That time together will always be waiting within each of our memories to come back and remind us that a call to service is primarily within us.

The Road to Nowhere

On the way back from Charlotte's farm, we had a chance to talk.

Charlotte remembered a strange highway that came to a dead end. There are warning signs, but the traffic is not required to exit the freeway at the last chance to do so. The road has been nicknamed "the road to nowhere."

On one of her curious trips, Charlotte went all the way to the end just to see if it was as people had stated. She came upon the end of the road that backs up to a thickly wooded area near Reading, Pennsylvania. Even though she knew that it was a dead-end road, she came upon it quite suddenly.

Appropriately, there is a sign at the end of the road informing you to take the paved path over the median to the other side of the road.

I often find that I can come upon dead ends in my life. There are early warnings and suggestions to take an alternate path. God lets me keep going on my highway at full speed right up to the end.

Much like that path to the other side of the highway, my "road to nowhere" has a roadblock with a sign telling me to turn back. I waste a lot of time continuing. On my road past the last exit, I have come close to running into the woods at the end.

There are documented accounts of people who go headfirst into the woods, expecting to find the rest of the road beyond the trees. They don't get far before having a major accident with fatal consequences.

How is your eyesight these days? Or better yet, do you even look for the exit signs? Some exits in life are fruitless, but others can be exciting. Are you watching for those signs that say, "Last exit before paying a toll"? Consider the price before continuing. And don't miss the last exit. You will have to take it eventually. Better to take it coming than returning, that is, if you make your way back at all.

A Hole in the Ground

It was a cool summer evening as the sun was setting over the freshly plowed field. Out in the distance, just beyond the first crest of the hill, was a hole about one hundred feet in diameter and several feet deep. Leading up to the craterlike artifact was the gravel driveway freshly laid. It was five years coming, but there it was. It was the first sign of site work on the plot of land that soon would become the promised land for our local congregation.

A cool breeze always does this to me. It reminds me of something deep in my past, something I had conveniently forgotten. Usually, this happens in the fall as the cool weather is welcoming in the winter, but today was different. It was the first day of summer, but the weather map looked like September. I took an afternoon stroll around the block and listened to the wind in the trees as I recalled one of God's promises seven years before.

In June, seven years ago, I moved to the Washington, DC area, all alone and unsure of my new surroundings. I asked God to make this feel like home to me. I didn't want to feel like a wanderer. He promised me that He would answer my request, but I didn't know when this would happen.

Now, seven years later, I am finally in a place that feels like home. My first two dwellings were apartments—not quite what I had in mind, but necessary nonetheless. As I approach my third year in my townhouse, I have a flower bed, a lawnmower, and several neighbors as close friends, and I finally planted some shrubs in the front yard. "Is this enough?" I asked the Lord as I walked past the pond with children playing on the swing sets in the distance.

Substance. That's what we need to realize that God is answering our requests. We are people of little faith. All along, we know in our hearts that the promise is being fulfilled, but to see it with our eyes or to hear it with our ears is refreshing. To the person searching for a job, it's the first paycheck. To an expectant couple, it is the first cry from their child. To a heartbroken single person, it is the words, "I love you."

For some, a simple hole in the ground will do. That's all I had. I wondered how long it would be before I became dissatisfied.

We Need You

Three simple words echoed in my heart and my mind as I buried my face in a pillow. God had spoken to me audibly. The turning point of an episode of my favorite TV show hung on those three words spoken with compassion and sincerity, "We need you."

To be needed is one of the basic desires that keeps us going even when all else seems to be lost. To be liked, to be unique, and to be loved are all feelings that give us life, but to hear those three simple words is what we all hope, pray, and long for.

I heard those words many times in my past, both to a group as well as directed toward me. But how can I even begin to tell you what those words meant to me at a time when I was feeling like I was inadequate, unaccepted, alone, and afraid that I was no longer able to do what I had been called to do?

There are times when responsibilities become overwhelming, when tasks are too complicated, and when life hardly seems worth the effort. There are times when you try your hardest, but somehow it just isn't good enough. That is the time when you need to hear a word of encouragement—not about how good a job you are doing but that you are the only one who can make things better for a dear friend or a loved one.

After I raised my head from the pillow and wiped the tears from my eyes, I realized that God had clearly articulated what so many of my dear friends and family members tried to say in their ways—ways that had not penetrated my overly sensitive, overly negative attitude that I felt toward myself—"Even in your current state, as inadequate as you may be (and feel), we need you."

But the question remained in my mind: "What was so special about me?" I needed the answer before I could move forward.

What Happened to Me?

If you look at the table of contents, you know that I married. I guess that's sufficient, but there's more to say.

I finished incorporating my Kirby chronicles into this book. It's going to take me longer to write the second half. I have a lot of things written down but not organized. I had no idea that I was going to write a book about my life until a few weeks ago. Amazingly, memories are coming back to me that were long lost.

I did not plan to wait until I was thirty-four to get married. I wasn't sure that I would ever get married, but it was always on the edge of my mind. I had married friends who were happy. I had married friends who were not happy. Was I supposed to wait until I was married to be happy? Could I be happy while I was single? Was being happy important?

I was happy some of the time, but joyful most of the time. I had struggles, but I enjoyed life. Sometimes, I felt like I was locked up and the key was thrown away. Then things changed and I wasn't sure why I didn't feel locked up anymore.

People looked at me and wondered when I would get married and who I would marry. Was there something wrong with me because I was not married? I didn't think so, but some people did.

At the time, I thought I was normal. I still think I was. I had single friends and some of them were female. I entertained the thought of marrying a few of them. Others, I knew would be just good friends.

Good friends come and good friends go. Most of my good friends were gone. One went to Sri Lanka, one went to Hawaii, and many left in the sunset.

Then something happened. It was a life-changing event. I don't remember the exact moment or day, but I realized the person that God created me to be. It was OK for people to help by speaking into my life, but I had to remain true to my calling.

It was a time of transition, but I wasn't sure how long it would be. I needed to be around people who could help me, not people who were trying to fix me.

PART IV

Married Life

CHAPTER 11

Am I Ready?

Ready for what?

Could it be time? The pastor at my church was concerned that the young adults were having fun but not concerned for life. He preached a sermon directed toward the singles who were in a serious relationship but were afraid to make a commitment. I thought it was a good sermon, but he didn't say anything about discernment. He had a list of things that the man should evaluate before he got married. I liked the list, but there was something missing.

I reviewed my notes from the sermon. If I evaluated my life exactly as he preached, I would have to conclude that God was displeased with me. According to his checklist, there was no reason why I should not be actively pursuing a mate. I was not.

There was nothing in the pastor's sermon directing the young men to ask the Lord for confirmation of any type. Some Christians believe that God is not concerned about who you marry and when. I found several verses in the Bible that addressed my concern. When I asked my dad for advice, he advised me to have a private conversation with the pastor. After our meeting, I asked the Lord to guide me to my next assignment.

My neighbor invited me to his church. I knew that I was in the right place because I needed a lot of help and there were plenty of people who could help me.

I had good trainers and good friends. One of my good friends became my best friend. Then I asked the question again, "Am I ready?"

The short answer was "no." Who is ever ready when they get married? There might be a few people in the world but I have not met them. If I do, I will recommend that they write a book. It will be a bestseller, guaranteed!

I was friends with Susan for about four years before we married. Each year, we learned more about each other and became better friends. I helped Susan with her math homework and her budget, and she made chocolate chip cookies for me. I knew we were becoming best friends because we were able to help each other.

When Susan and I considered the possibility of getting married, we spent a lot of time talking about what it might be like if we were married. We called these sessions "What if?" We knew people who decided to get married before they talked about any of the crucial decisions. We didn't want that to happen to us. What questions should we consider and how long would it take?

Susan and I were married later in life. We knew there was a possibility that we may have natural children, but it didn't seem likely. We discussed adopting children. We both had a heart for children who needed homes. I also had a concern for young boys who didn't have a father. I mentored boys in our church that only had a mother. Some people understood why I spent time with these boys, but others did not. I wasn't hiding anything and I did not need to convince anybody what I was doing was the will of the Lord.

After we talked to a few of our friends who had adopted children, our hearts were more drawn to children who were orphans.

There were other important discussions as well. We agreed that Susan would be a stay-at-home mom while the kids were young.

Susan had a cockatiel. The bird's cage was on a table next to her phone. When the phone rang, the bird said hello before Susan answered. I knew nothing about birds. I understood cats and dogs, but what do you do with a bird? Susan had several birds before Winsome, so I deferred to her on anything related to the bird. I

REMOVE THE LOCK 🔒

found out later that the bird was my pet too. I had to understand Winsome, and Winsome had to learn to understand me. Winsome and I became singing buddies.

When I asked Susan to marry me, we were best friends. Why would I want to marry somebody who wasn't my best friend?

It was no surprise to any of our friends when Susan and I were engaged. It was no surprise to Susan's mom either. In her mind, we were married long before I asked Susan to be my wife. They had a close relationship and talked a lot about what was happening in their lives.

My dad was surprised. Many times, he asked me on the phone if there was a special girl in my life. I talked about the single women that I was interested in. I was cautious about saying anything specific about Susan. I wasn't trying to hide anything from my dad. I didn't want him to draw a conclusion before I believed that Susan was the woman for me. I was too cautious in my discussions with my dad.

After we were engaged, Susan and I visited her mom in Syracuse, New York. We also visited my family in Wilmington, Delaware.

Susan's cousins were a different matter. The guys were friendly and treated me with respect, but it took some time for me to get used to their sense of humor. Some people think I still don't understand them.

On that joyous day when I asked Susan if she would be my wife, I was surprised at her initial response.

I asked, "Susan, will you marry me?"

Susan said, "Is this another what-if?"

I responded, "No, this is not a what-if. I am asking you to be my wife."

Susan said excitedly, "Yes!"

Susan and I had a common interest in poetry. We also enjoyed trying to understand early English. I wrote a poem for Susan in my attempt to write like some of the famous poets of old. I forgot this poem until recently as I was going through my journals.

Till Heaven's Open Door
12/22/92

What is thine thought
That tho dost keep
From all thine friends today—

A heart of gold,
A thought so pure
That only tho canst say.

For in thine heart
And in thine soul
Tho hardly canst relay,

How much thee care
For thine sweetheart
Who art with thee this day.

So on mine knee
I ask of thee
Could'est tho marry me—

For in mine heart
And in mine soul
Is room for only thee.

And with God's grace
I pledge to thee
To be thy true'est more—

To be thine mate
And be thine love
Till heaven's open door.

Susan and I wrote our vows in the form of a responsive poem. I wrote a line, and Susan wrote a response. The rhyming scheme and tempo were like Dr. Seuss's poems. The pastor agreed to let us read the poem, but he insisted that we have traditional vows as well. One of our friends thought that it was funny that Susan included her bird in the poem. I thought that it was appropriate.

What I Know

The Lord's provision has never been a question. There are things that I know and there are things that I'm still trying to understand. When I graduated from high school, I knew that the Lord was going to provide for me and my family. I knew that He would guide me into a career path that would give me the opportunities I needed.

When I became an employee of IBM, I thought that I would never have to look for a job. My dad worked for DuPont, and he was confident that his job would be secure if he was able to perform at an acceptable level. I believed the same for myself.

The IBM Corporation had the reputation of being one of the finest companies in America. It survived many financial challenges. IBM never laid off a single employee. From the top level down, every employee was respected. If the company changed directions, management believed that it was their responsibility to reassign their employees.

I was not trusting in my employer. I was trusting in my Lord. If anything happened to the corporation or my job, I knew that God had a plan to take care of me and those I was responsible for. I knew that with all my heart, but sometimes, my heart was not able to convince my mind of the truth.

When I asked Susan to marry me, I had been employed by the IBM Corporation for almost eight years. I had plenty of challenges, but I always had a testimony of how God's goodness brought me through.

We planned to get married in September of 1993. In May,

we were ahead of schedule. Most of the planning was completed, including our honeymoon to England and Scotland. The economy was still on the downturn, but I had no fears. There were rumors that IBM was taking drastic measures to reorganize. Even when our managers told us that IBM was going to lay off employees, I was sure that my job was secure.

If I trusted in what I knew, the layoffs would have not affected me. However, I struggled when I was notified that I was on the list. No one could tell me why I was laid off. That also should not have been a concern, but it added to my hurt. I controlled my emotions while I was at the office, but as soon as I arrived home, I started to cry. I didn't want to tell Susan, but I had to. I knew we would get through it. Susan became my greatest cheerleader and she never stopped encouraging me.

That evening, I called my dad and told him what happened. He asked me if Susan and I were still planning to get married. I said, "I don't know a lot of things, but I do know that Susan and I are supposed to get married on schedule." My dad was surprised, but he was supportive.

Even though IBM laid off 40 percent of the employees in my division in one day, they still gave a nice severance pay. Since I worked eight years for the company, my severance pay was equivalent to four months of my regular pay. I needed a job, but I had money to carry me through.

I applied for several jobs during the summer. I started my new job two weeks before Susan and I were married. My only request was for two weeks of unpaid leave for my honeymoon. My new employer granted my request.

CHAPTER 12

Marriage

Our Wedding

If I could repeat just one day of my life, I would pick my wedding day. Even with all the things that didn't go as we planned, it was an amazing day. I have nothing written down because I don't need anything to remind me of the details. I don't have a good memory, but I reserved a special space for that day. That memory is guarded in a way that it cannot be removed or tampered with.

God's blessing was on that day. Every day in September is not a perfect day, but most good days of the year are in that month. That's why Susan and I picked September to be married. The first Saturday was Labor Day weekend, so we rejected that day. The next Saturday was the eleventh. For the first seven years of our marriage, we joyously celebrated on that day. On our eighth anniversary, we were at church praying for God's mercy and protection for our country.

My brother, Bob, was my best man. He helped me drop my car at the hotel where Susan and I would stay the night after the wedding. I was not going to drive Susan to the hotel, so I needed our car there.

I wanted everything to be perfect. I prayed for a beautiful day, and it was. The sun was shining, there was a light breeze, and the temperature was in the mid-seventies. It was a perfect day for Susan and me to get married.

If I had prayed for all the other details, we may have avoided some of the mishaps. God uses struggles to help us lean into him when things are not as we expect.

Susan was aware of several things that were not going as planned, but she didn't let anybody tell me. Susan knew that I didn't need any extra stress. Even then, she was looking out for my well-being.

The person who was hired to do the hair for the women did not show up, and the person who was hired to do the makeup for the women did not show up. It was not a tragedy because Susan's cousin, Nancy, was amazing at both.

We asked good friends to be our wedding day administrators. They did an excellent job as expected. If they made a mistake, I never found out.

As was tradition, we had a rehearsal the day before the ceremony. Everyone knew exactly what they were supposed to do, including the ring bearer who walked by himself holding the ring. He followed instructions perfectly. The video captured Matthew's smile when he handed the ring to the best man. Some couples get nervous and don't let the ring bearer carry the actual ring. We could not do that to Matthew. Even at a young age, he was a soldier who knew how to follow orders. I wished that I was ready at that age. My life would have been significantly different.

We were entertained by a bagpiper while we waited for the limousine to arrive. Some of the guests danced to the music.

When the limousine did not arrive on time, we received a message that the driver was involved in an accident on the beltway. He was not going to be available to take the bride and groom to their hotel.

We did not have a backup plan. My dad and stepmom graciously volunteered to take the happy couple to their honeymoon suite.

At least half of the people who attended our wedding ceremony were immediately available to help with anything that did not go as expected. I should not have had any concern whatsoever, but I was nervous the whole time.

When I viewed the video of our wedding, I looked like I was scared to death. I was overjoyed to marry Susan, but I realized what a great responsibility it was to be a husband and father. I not only wanted to be the best example possible, but I wanted to be better than possible.

Our Honeymoon

I'm sitting in Chick-fil-A. This was one of our favorite places to eat. We each bought a chicken sandwich and a frosted coffee. Susan asked me to get a brownie. She didn't want one for herself. She wanted to share mine. Many times, I asked her why she didn't want her brownie, but she never gave me an answer.

As I always did, today, I broke my brownie in half and said, "This half is for me and you can have the bigger half. I need you to help me write this chapter."

As expected, I didn't get a response. I closed my eyes and wondered what Susan would say. I believe she would say, "I can be your cheerleader. I can encourage you, but it must come from your heart of gold. You still have it, so I know you're going to be able to write. And it's going to be fantastic."

Our trip to England and Scotland started in the middle of the week after our wedding day. While we waited, we relaxed and unwrapped our wedding gifts.

When we arrived in England, we changed our watches to match the local time. We ignored our feeling of jet lag and enjoyed our first day in London. As we were considering dinner, we asked a local for a recommendation. The suggested restaurant sounded wonderful to Susan and me. We were worn out and happy that the instructions sounded like a short walk down the street.

We thought we missed the restaurant, so we asked another friendly person for directions. He said, "You are almost there. Just to the top of the hill."

We did not know what that meant; however, we were hopeful that we would arrive before we collapsed.

After another unexpectedly long time, we decided to ask another local. Amazingly, we received almost the same response. We asked each other, "How much further can it possibly be?"

When we finally arrived, the restaurant was nice, but not what we expected. It reminded us of restaurants in the States. We wanted a different experience but were so tired and hungry that we didn't care.

After dinner, Susan said that we needed a way to get to the hotel that was not walking. A kind man told us that we could wait for the next bus on the other side of the street. The bus took us to our hotel. That was a good plan.

Our tour officially started the next morning in the breakfast area of the hotel. After a good night's sleep, Susan and I enjoyed getting to know our fellow travelers. The breakfast was a new experience for me. Before we got married, Susan and a friend toured England, so she knew what to expect.

The tour was well organized. We spent a large amount of our time riding on the bus from town to town. The tour guide told us a lot of interesting facts.

So that no one would feel like they were being cheated, the tour guide implemented an interesting way to determine where we would sit on the bus each day. From day two forward, every person had an assigned seat. It was simple to determine where to sit. You remembered the seat you were sitting in the previous day and moved four seats counterclockwise in the bus.

After a few days, the people who were sitting in the front seat on the left side found themselves sitting close to the back on the same side. The left side transitioned to the right side in the back. The people who were on the right side of the bus moved four seats forward each day. There were a lot of things that I don't remember, but I could never forget riding on the bus. I've never experienced anything like it.

Each little town in England and Scotland is unique. Some towns have not changed in hundreds of years. Other towns have new developments next to century-old buildings.

As we were listening to a group singing Christian songs, Susan remarked that some of the songs were familiar to her. The songs were written by one of the well-known songwriters for our group of churches in the States.

Susan loved to work with ancestry records. I told her that one of my ancestors was an earl in the town of Lauder, Scotland. The tour we chose allowed us time to drive from Edinburgh to Lauder.

I drove our rental car, even though I had never driven in England before. Driving on the left side of the road was a huge challenge. I would not have been able to do it if my chief cheerleader and encourager were not sitting next to me. "Stay left, stay left" was her continual instruction.

Lauder is a tiny town, and the castle is next to the town. A woman in the gift shop was also a tour guide in the castle. She told us that Tuesday was the day when the castle was not open for tours. We were disappointed that we had not carefully considered the day that we would be in Edinburgh.

I drove to the site of the original castle. There wasn't much left of it, but we found rocks that were probably used for a doorway. There was a ninety-degree notch out of one end of one of the rocks that we brought home. I kept the one with the notch and gave the other one to my dad. I still have my castle rock safely stored in my garage.

Each morning, just before we ate breakfast in our hotel, we put our luggage outside our door. The hotel staff put the luggage on the bus.

One morning, I was wondering why the pick-up people were late. As I was standing on the inside of the door, I heard one of the porters say, "This one is really heavy. It feels like it has rocks in it."

I was tempted to open the door and say that he was right, but the look on Susan's face told me that it was not a good idea.

It rains a lot in England and Scotland in the fall. The only day it rained was when we were in the Lake District. We had a few short opportunities to get out of the bus to take pictures. While we were at Loch Ness, everyone looked intently for the monster. No one was able to produce a picture that was convincing, so we concluded that the monster did not like rain.

Susan was like her mom. They always looked for special deals.

Her mom called them "rake-offs." It's hard to get a rake-off when everything is paid upfront. Somehow, Susan and I received special consideration because we were on our honeymoon. Every other day, our room was nicer than everybody else's.

I want to write more about our honeymoon. Some things are hard for me to write. I know what I want to say, but I can't come up with the words. It was a fantastic dream that I thought would never end.

CHAPTER 13

Children

Adopting Our Children

No one likes to read about themselves, especially when you are not sure what the author is going to say. So Joseph and Julia, I won't be offended if you skip the next few pages. I can't leave you out of my story because you are a special part of who I am. This is not a story about you, so don't be surprised if I leave things out that you think should be in this book.

Long before I imagined that I would be married, I had a heart for children who were left behind or mistreated. I wondered if I could do a better job. I wondered if I could help even a little bit. Could I demonstrate some good qualities of who our Heavenly Father is?

I mentioned in a previous chapter that I looked like I was scared to death just before I married Susan. My friends knew me well. They knew that what was on my face was not what was in my heart. The same was true when I was considering how I could care for little boys who didn't have a father. Many people misunderstood my motivations. They thought it was a way for me to get in good favor with the boy's mom. That was never the case.

When Susan and I began sharing our hearts, adopting children was important to both of us. Susan understood me better than I understood myself. Also, I knew that she wanted to be a mom. Even if she wasn't a mom, she still wanted to care for children.

Before we were married, I sat by myself and cried because I didn't know how to do what my heart was leading me to do. It wasn't impossible for a single person to adopt a child. I knew a few people who did, but I couldn't see doing that myself. I knew I was going to need a lot of help.

In Russia, orphans are in an orphanage. They stay there until someone adopts them. If they get to a certain age, they must leave the orphanage. Some have nowhere to go and no one to help them.

In the United States, most orphans start in foster homes. Some children eventually get adopted by the foster parents, but most of them don't. The assumption is that the child is in a safe place until an adoptive family can be found for them. Sometimes that works and sometimes it doesn't. I don't want to judge the system in this country, but I don't like it.

I'm not saying that other countries handle orphans perfectly. Every orphan is confused and hurt because of what happened in their life. As an adoptive family, the best we can do is show them our love.

When Susan and I married, we were considering adopting children. The desire was strong in both of us. We knew several families who had adopted children from other countries. We pursued foreign adoption as well.

We were not sure how many children we were going to adopt, so we requested approval to adopt up to three children under the age of ten at the same time. Some countries require you to adopt siblings together. If we were called to adopt one child and there was a sibling in the orphanage system, we would need to adopt the siblings together. We knew some families who did that.

Waiting for Joseph

Susan and I agonized over the many choices for adopting children. Every option had easy and hard components, pros and cons, different timelines, different costs, and different risks.

Our final decision was not a logical one. There was no logical best decision. It wasn't like buying a car or a house. We were not looking for convenience, prestige, personal preference, or financial affordability.

Adopting a child is a matter of the heart. We were compelled to use a specific agency. We were given videos of the children that we had some interest in. As we watched the children interact with each other and the caretakers in the orphanage, our hearts leaped within our chests for a specific child. We knew that the child was destined to be a member of our family.

The challenges started when we switched from our hearts to our minds. There were plenty of things we had to carefully consider. It wasn't a matter of whether we would change our minds, but convincing our minds that our hearts had made the correct decision.

When I felt in my heart that Susan was the person who was selected to be my life mate, part of my assurance came directly from Susan. When Susan and I chose a child to adopt, we did not get a confirmation from the child. How could we know that the child would accept us as parents?

The screening that was required by law only validated that Susan and I would be good parents—not necessarily good parents for the child that we decided to adopt. We were adopting a child who already had several years of experience that we were only partially aware of. To adopt a child under these conditions is not a logical thing to do, but you cannot adopt a child with your mind. It must be from your heart.

The child we chose to adopt was in an orphanage in Russia. When I was a child, Russia was not a friend. It took some time for me to recognize the good things about Russia. Once I was old enough to understand politics and reasons why people don't like countries in general, I changed my mind quickly. I have nothing against the people of Russia. Most of the reasons for our diplomatic issues are not applicable to most of the people in those countries.

We selected Joseph in January. We were expecting to go to Russia to adopt him in March. During this time, Russia made changes in its adoption process. One of the changes that was made just before we left required Joseph to be put on a list of available orphans. Russian parents were given priority in selecting children to adopt. If a child was not adopted within six months, he was released for a foreign adoption.

Waiting was harder than anything that we did. There was never a time when we questioned whether Joseph would be our child. It was a heart-wrenching delay.

Susan often said to me, "I want my boy, and I want him now." She knew in her mind that it was not possible, but her heart still wanted the boy that was promised to her. I also struggled with waiting. I don't remember mentioning this to Susan, but I wondered if there would be an additional delay. Thankfully, there was not.

Adopting Joseph

I never liked traveling. I still don't. One of my project leaders loved to drive a car. When he and his wife went on vacations, he drove the whole time and his wife enjoyed being the passenger. Some people like going on cruises. Some people like flying in airplanes. Some people like riding in a camper across the country. That's fine for them, but I like staying close to home.

Most of the adventure things that I don't like now were missing in my childhood. Is that a good or a bad thing? I'm not sure. I miss opportunities because I'm hesitant to do things that are foreign to me. Should I be more willing to take on new challenges?

These were going through my mind just before we left to adopt Joseph. I struggled with going to England and Scotland for our honeymoon. Susan picked up on it, but she didn't know the extent of my hesitancy to travel.

Being in a country like England where people spoke my language was helpful. The new experience of driving on the left-hand side of the road gave me some stress, but having Susan next to me relieved most of it.

I knew that going to Russia would bring unexpected things. Even though most of the people could speak English, I was still concerned.

Susan had experience traveling overseas, so she encouraged me. But there was still much to be dealt with. Even though Russia was a friendly nation, I had concerns for our safety. Military guards were stationed at the entrance of most buildings in the cities. We had to show our passports and visas everywhere we went. We never had any problems, but we always had to prove that we had a good reason for being where we were.

Joseph lived in an orphanage outside the city of Saint Petersburg. We adopted Joseph in the month of October. The days were short and the temperatures were moderate.

We weren't by ourselves. We traveled with a couple from California who were adopting a girl who was in the orphanage with Joseph. It was nice to have friends during most of our trip. We had a couple from the United States, and the kids traveled with someone that they knew from their orphanage.

We were in Russia for just one week, which I thought was amazing. A Russian contact had taken care of most of the administrative part of the adoption before we arrived. She worked with our adoption agency for several years. When the adoption process changed, she kept up. She did not work for the adoption agency directly. She was a contractor, and we paid for her services in US dollars. We were happy that we could do that instead of having to exchange our dollars for Russian rubles. There were other things that we had to pay for with rubles.

Everything related to the adoption process was completed in Saint Petersburg; however, we had to go to the US Embassy in

Moscow to get a visa for our child to enter the United States. Even though we had officially adopted our child in Russia, the child was still a Russian citizen. Our embassy had no concerns about giving us a visa for our adopted child. It was just another inconvenience. We took an overnight train from Saint Petersburg to Moscow, which was slow and rocked back and forth. We were not able to sleep during the ride, so we were exhausted the next morning.

In Moscow, we stayed at the home of a precious lady who loved children. Joseph told her that we did not speak Russian but he would teach us. Joseph thought that the game was for us to learn Russian, but he was also learning English. The lady said a word in Russian and then the equivalent in English. Joseph repeated the two words. Then Joseph came into the room where we were and spoke the Russian and English words for us. We repeated the Russian and English words. Joseph thought that that was a lot of fun.

We were only in Moscow for one day. Our flight home was originally scheduled to allow for an extra day in Moscow in case there was an unexpected delay.

When everything went exactly as planned, we wanted to take a flight home the next morning instead of waiting the extra day. The driver took us to the airline business office in downtown Moscow. That's where they did everything. There was no place in the airport to help with flight arrangements.

When we arrived at the building, we went through the security checkpoint. Russian citizens went through one door and everybody else went through a different door. We thought that the Payne family was going to be the holdup. After seeing our US passports and visas, the security guard allowed us to go through with our adopted child.

We waited for several minutes for our driver. I realized that our driver was being held up by security. He was having a hard time convincing the guard that he should come into the building. I went to the guard who was talking to our driver. I asked to make a petition for my driver. The guard said that it was OK for him to stay outside and wait for us. I was able to convince the guard that he was more than just our driver. I said that he was hired to be my guide and translator. When I said that I needed him to help me with the flight arrangements, the guard allowed the driver to come in. Later, when I was thinking about the incident, I wondered how I had enough courage to do that. The answer was that I did not have courage. I just did it.

Our driver understood the children. He had twin boys about the age of Joseph. Joseph loved to sing songs. He was singing in Russian, so we had no idea what he was saying. We asked the driver to translate the song. The driver said, "It's just a little boy rambling." We still wanted to know what the song was about, but we never found out.

Early in the morning, as we were going to the airport, the driver pulled over and stopped the car. He said, "Everything is OK. I must check something."

Susan and I were nervous, but it took less than a minute for the driver to open the hood and make some minor adjustments. Earlier, he told us that with his brother's help, he built his car out of used parts. It was like his baby. He knew exactly the noises it made and when it needed attention. The car never broke down, so we had to believe that he knew what he was doing.

While we were standing in a long line at the airport, Joseph was antsy. Susan was holding his hand, and he felt like it wasn't necessary. Joseph still spoke nothing but Russian, and we understood little of what he said. One of the ladies who was in the line with us asked if we knew what our son was saying. We said we did not.

The woman said, "Your son says that if you let go of his hand, he will not run away. He will stay next to his mother."

Susan and I had a short discussion and decided that it was OK for Joseph to walk next to Susan without being held. It was a good decision. Joseph followed instructions even though he knew little English. He picked up a few phrases. The one I used most of the time was, "Stay with Mama." Mama is almost universal. It means mother in Russian. He needed to stay with Papa when we went to the restroom. Joseph got that one too. He was a quick learner. We were glad of that. When I taught him some American

Sign Language, Joseph enjoyed acting, so he thought that it was a game.

Susan homeschooled Joseph for the first year. There were other homeschooled children from Russia that Joseph enjoyed interacting with. They had a co-op that was sponsored by the Christian school that was run by our church.

The neighborhood children wondered why he did not sound like he was from Russia. We told them that Joseph was learning English from us, so he pronounced words the way we did.

Adopting Julia

Susan and I learned a lot from our experience of adopting our first child from Russia. However, no two children are the same and no two adoptions are the same.

Two years after adopting Joseph, we were ready to adopt our second child. Since the experience with the adoption agency went well, we used it again.

Susan wanted a little girl, but we also considered having a younger brother for Joseph. Once again, we thought through the options, but the final decision came from our hearts.

By 1998, the Russian economy was beginning to stabilize, but we were still encouraged to go to the bank frequently in Russia to exchange our dollars for rubles.

The Russian people are friendly and polite. When we entered the bank lobby, a gentleman identified himself as the one who entered the bank just before us. People don't stand in a long line like the United States. The line to approach the tellers consisted of three or four people. Each person watched the person who arrived in the lobby just before them. I went to the line behind the person that was my predecessor.

We were given information about clothes sizes for our daughter that we were adopting. Unfortunately, the translation into our sizes did not match well. When we arrived in Russia, we realized that the clothes we had for Julia would not fit. Our Russian assistant took us to a clothes store immediately after we picked her up from the orphanage. Russian law states that if you were a business with a permanent location, you must use rubles for all your transactions.

The same was true for the restaurant in our hotel. Fortunately, the restaurant was willing to take our credit card and charged us the appropriate amount in rubles. The credit card company handled the conversion for us.

We still wanted to know how much money we were spending on our dinner. I knew the current conversion between rubles and US dollars. Susan asked me to estimate the bill in US dollars. I thought I knew what I was doing, but the amount was so low that I couldn't believe it. They charged us for everything, including bottled water and butter for our bread.

Our children changed their minds and ordered more than once. I was sure it was going to be a huge bill. I was amazed when the total for dinner was slightly over twenty US dollars. We were in a restaurant in a five-star hotel in downtown Moscow.

We were told that we did not have to tip the waiter, but we were free to do so in any way we wanted to. When I offered the waiter a single one-dollar bill, he was overjoyed.

There was a snowstorm in Saint Petersburg the week before we arrived. This was typical for December, and we were pleasantly surprised that the temperature was not below zero.

We were standing in a parking lot that had been plowed. There was a delay getting into the van. Joseph thought that it would be fun to have a snowball fight. We were sure that Julia was familiar with snow, but she was unsure about playing with her dad. Joseph was no longer speaking Russian, but the children had their way of communicating.

Joseph initiated a snowball fight with me. I threw a snowball back at him. Julia was hesitant, but Joseph encouraged her. When she threw a snowball at me, I laughed and threw one back at her. She knew that this was an acceptable game to play with Papa.

A recent change in the Russian adoption process required the adoptive parents to appear before a court to petition for the adoption.

Our representative told us that the court process was required by law, but everyone already knew that the judge was going to approve the request. We would not have been called to court if the judge was unsure of the decision that he was going to make.

Most professionals in Russia, which would include judges and those in government positions, spoke English well enough that a translator was not necessary. However, Russian law requires that all court hearings be held using the Russian language only. It was permitted to have a translator, but everything had to be spoken in the Russian language.

Our representative had performed the service many times before we arrived. She knew exactly what the judge was going to say and translated almost as fast as he was speaking. I represented the Payne family and was given a script of what questions would be asked and appropriate responses by me. I was nervous, but I trusted my Russian representative.

There was a testimony from the director of Julia's orphanage. She said that we were good parents. She used as evidence the presence of Joseph who had been adopted two years earlier. He was well-adapted to our family and society. She said that Joseph and Julia had already bonded as brother and sister.

Close to the end of the trial, the judge left the courtroom for a short time to consider all the evidence. When he returned, he gave the judgment that we were acceptable parents for the adoption, so he approved the request.

The night before we left Saint Petersburg to go to Moscow, we ordered hard-boiled eggs for the next morning. Julia did not understand why she could not eat her hard-boiled egg for dinner. She was pleasantly surprised when she had her hard-boiled egg with warm tea on the train ride just before we arrived in Moscow. I have a picture of her smile. We didn't need her to say anything.

We knew what to expect when we arrived at the US Embassy to request a visa for Julia. Since Joseph was already a citizen of the United States, he was carrying a US passport and visa.

When we arrived home, Julia started learning English from

her brother and mother. I would guess that most of the English she learned was from Joseph. She learned English so fast that I was embarrassed when I talked to my dad. I told him on the phone that Julia had not learned enough English to have a conversation with him. She had only been in the United States for about three weeks. My dad said that he wanted to talk to his granddaughter anyway.

I sat next to Julia while she was talking to her grandpa. It was not a long conversation as expected, but she did not need any help. I could tell that the questions that my dad was asking were simple. Julia said things like, "I like playing with my brother" and "Mama gave me a pretty dress."

When Julia handed the phone back to me, my dad said, "I thought you told me that Julia did not know English."

I said, "She surprised me. I guess Joseph is a better teacher than I thought he was. She must be learning a lot while they play."

The Birthday Party

Our house was at the end of a long street, and we were bordered by a park in the back. Deer were regular visitors to our yard. They ate almost everything, even the rock-hard fruit that fell from a tree at our front door.

Our holly plants were almost exempt from our munching neighbors. I was amazed that they could eat holly leaves because they had pointy leaves. One winter when we had a lot of snow, our holly plants barely survived through the desperation of the deer.

I love all of God's creatures, but I am less loving toward the ones that eat all my plants. Anytime I said something against the deer, our kids got upset, and they did not want to hear that deer were hunted.

Occasionally, a deer hunter asked permission to stalk the deer from the tall trees in our backyard. I always said "no" for multiple reasons, the greatest being that there were children in our family and neighborhood.

We had a great yard for parties. We planned a birthday party

95

for our daughter. There would be horse riding and lots of outdoor games.

The morning before the party, I saw a strange pickup truck parked across the street. I am always thinking the worst. For me, on this day, the worst thing to deal with would be a deer hunter. The thought entered my mind, but it was just too unbelievable. I asked myself, "How could my neighbor across the street agree to have a deer hunter in his trees with my kids close by?"

I kept an eye on the truck for about an hour. There was no activity near the truck. Even if it was a deer hunter, he would be gone by that hour. I heard that the best time to hunt deer was in the early morning. It was about 11:00 a.m., and our party was scheduled for 1:00 p.m.

I asked Susan what I should do. We agreed that if it was a hunter, he could not remain when the children arrived for the party.

I went to the edge of the trees in my neighbor's yard and called out, "Is there a deer hunter in the trees?"

I heard the response, "Yes. I am here."

I said, "I live across the street. I need to talk to you."

He said, "I will be right down."

I realized that I had about one to two minutes before I had to confront this man. What was I going to say? What could I say? He wasn't on my property. I guessed that he had permission from the owner.

I spent my whole life trying to be a peacemaker. I wanted to answer in a kind, loving way. I wanted to be a good example for my children. I wanted to be a good example for my neighbors. I wanted to love my neighbor who had a deer hunter in his tree.

Life is not always fair. Many things in my life were not fair. Often, I sat by myself and thought about the difficult times I went through. Those were all in the past, so I thought. Was I still affected in some way by the things that happened to me?

When I wanted to be a math teacher to make a difference, I could not because I wouldn't be able to make enough money to support my family.

When I tried to get a master's degree to stay in the education field, I couldn't see myself taking some of the required courses, so I gave up my dream of being an educator.

When my heart reached out to young boys who didn't have a father, I was misunderstood. People thought that I was manipulating the situation so that the mother would like me.

When I believed that God wanted me to stay single to be a positive influence on the singles in my church, the pastor thought I missed my calling. He said that I should be aggressively pursuing someone to marry.

I waited patiently for the perfect wife. When I found her, I treated her respectfully until the appointed time when we would be married.

When I had no idea how we would have enough money to adopt two children with my salary, I waited for the right time. God came through for us with the finances that we needed.

When Susan and I knew in our hearts which children we should adopt, we tolerated the changes that the Russian government was doing with its adoption process.

We had a beautiful family, a peaceful neighborhood, and lots of friends to come to a birthday party for our precious daughter. I had a difficult decision. Would I be kind and lose this opportunity for my child or would I make a demand so forcefully that the hunter would leave or attack me?

All this was happening in one to two minutes. It shouldn't have to be this way. I worked hard to unlock the locks. I tried to stay out of the prisons that my life was trying to put me in. However, I was trapped once again. Would the locked door slam on me or would I find that the door no longer had a lock on it?

I stood face-to-face with a middle-aged man. I knew that he had the right to do what he was doing. I needed a way to convince him to voluntarily leave.

I said, "Do you have permission to hunt deer from this tree?"

The man said, "Yes. The owner of the property gave me

permission to hunt from this position. I usually hunt early in the morning, but I was delayed today."

I said, "I cannot force you to leave, but I appeal to you as a father of young children who are going to have a birthday party in about two hours in my front yard. I will do my best to keep the children on my side of the street. However, it is not going to be easy for me to do that. And if my children find out that you were hunting deer across the street, they will be frantic. I appeal to you as a father. Please leave now so that I don't have to deal with this difficult situation."

The man said, "I feel your heart of love for your children. I will leave."

I said, "I have no authority to tell you to stop hunting from this position, but I ask you to find a better place where there will not be any children in danger."

The man said, "I will consider your request."

I did not see the man again or his truck parked across the street. He may have come early in the morning before anybody in my family woke, but I considered it an acceptable solution to my problem.

As I look back on the situation, I don't know if I was successful in removing that lock.

CHAPTER 14

Home

Serenity

One definition for serenity is, "the state of being calm, peaceful, and untroubled."

Could this be attained in this life? I believed it could. There was a time when I was close.

Our house was like a retreat center but with a few interruptions. Our screened-in back porch was protected from the strong winds by our garage that extended behind the back of our house. I loved to sit on the swinging loveseat even if no one was sitting with me. My wife sat with me on occasion, but our cat, Tokyo, attended to me more often.

Tokyo was a typical independent cat. She was slow to arrive in her state of serenity. She was always on alert even when it seemed like she was calm. My morning routine included her most of the time.

My favorite time of the year is the fall. I love a cool breeze and listening to birds singing. Each day gave me a different view into our backyard as the leaves were changing and falling off the trees. When the wind was blowing, I did not feel it. I could see the effect it was having on the trees in the woods behind my house. The gentle voice of God was in the sound of the wind as it went by.

Most evenings in the fall were pleasant, even if it was warm during the middle of the day. After dinner, my wife and I walked slowly down the street. Some days, we walked about halfway down our street, which measured approximately three quarters of a mile. On other days, we would only go to the second house and turn around. Even then, we both knew that Susan was feeling the effects of her diminishing health.

Tokyo did not want to miss anything. Sometimes, she watched and walked away. Other times, she insisted on being a central part of the activity. We never asked Tokyo to walk with us, but she frequently did.

I knew that Tokyo was wondering why we walked slowly. She scampered ahead and waited for us to catch up. If she saw something interesting, she observed it for a while.

Our neighbors were friendly. The family that lived two doors down had two children close to the ages of our children. They interacted some, but not as much as we were hoping.

On one of our walks, the woman asked if we would come in for a short time. While we were inside the house, Tokyo waited patiently for us. When we continued our walk, Tokyo was ready to go.

The neighbors were intrigued by our cat. They wondered why she stayed so close to us, even though she was not on a leash. I was thinking that she had the motherly instinct to watch after her charges.

I loved working in the yard. I learned so much from my dad. His passion outstripped mine. In my eyes, he was amazing. When I had a smaller yard, I could keep up. Our new larger property was filled with beautiful beds that had shrubs and flowering trees. Because the deer ate almost every flower that existed, we only had a few varieties in our garden.

I bought a riding lawnmower, and I enjoyed my rides around the yard. It was difficult in the spring when the grass grew fast. I loved trimming the shrubs if I didn't run into a wasp nest. Even though we had a contract with a pest control company, the wasps found a way to build a nest between the service times.

We had an in-ground pool in the backyard. It was a lot of work, but also a lot of fun for our kids when they were young. I loved sitting on the side and listening to my kids say, "Look at me now." Julia swam like a fish. She was always calling her brother to jump in the pool with her. He was more interested in cleaning the skimmers so he could rescue bugs and frogs.

We had a basketball net next to our driveway. When I was younger, I loved playing basketball. My friend had a basketball net at his house. I was excited when I realized that we would have one at our house. Our children enjoyed my trick shots. They thought that I was a superstar. I tried to explain to them how long it took me to practice the shot before I could make it reliably. They didn't care. They said that it was fun to watch me.

When we bought our house, there was a pool table in the basement. I loved to play pool even more than I loved to play basketball. When I practiced, I was good. The only thing I had to fight was my anxiousness. My childhood friend taught me a lot about playing pool. I knew how to make the shots, but I often took the shot before I was ready. Sometimes, I missed easy shots. Our children learned to play and enjoyed playing with me. Susan loved to watch but didn't play often.

Susan's mom lived with us in a ground-floor in-law suite. Our children loved to be with their grandma. I remembered what it was like to live with my grandmother. I'm glad that my children had that opportunity to get to know her.

During this time, there were many trials and tribulations. I remember some, but thankfully, I forgot a lot. My pleasant memories help to keep me from being trapped in my loneliness.

Rescuing Tokyo

Tokyo is our daughter's cat. Close to bedtime, Julia called her cat to come into the house. Sometimes, Tokyo wanted to stay out and prowl.

If Tokyo wanted to come in and no one was available to open the door, she climbed a tree next to the garage and jumped onto the garage roof. Julia's room was at the front of the house. There was a small ledge outside each of the windows. The garage roof was about ten feet from Julia's window ledge. The ledge was four inches wide. Cats are amazing jumpers, but I never understood how Tokyo was able to perform that jump.

Tokyo cried and scratched the window until Julia let her in. Sometimes during the day, Tokyo would get impatient and jump on the window ledge. Tokyo sat there until Julia came into her room. The neighbors saw Tokyo sitting on the ledge and were concerned. They asked if we knew that our poor cat was stranded on the window ledge.

When Tokyo arrived at our house, the next-door neighbor had two cats. Tokyo was intimidated by one of them and stayed close to home. When both neighbor cats were no longer there, Tokyo believed that her space had expanded.

In addition to the times that Tokyo walked with Susan and me, she also wandered off by herself. Two dogs lived in the house that was three doors away from us. The dogs were almost never in the yard.

One day, Tokyo was on an adventure and wandered into the dog's territory. The dogs chased Tokyo up a tall tree. The dogs were brought into the house. The neighbor called us and apologized for allowing her dogs to run without a leash. She said the dogs chased Tokyo up a tree, and she didn't want to come down.

I went to the neighbor's house and talked to the owner. She apologized again several times. I told her that it was OK. Tokyo had no business being in their yard, but I still had to figure out a way to convince Tokyo to come down. The people had a deck in their backyard that was next to the large tree. I brought a ladder from my house and I climbed close to the first large branch of the tree. Tokyo walked down the large branch. She was almost close enough for me to grab her.

Tokyo did not like me picking her up. Now that she was frightened, she was even less willing to allow me to hold her. I was wondering what was going through her mind. She probably thought that I was incapable of safely carrying her down the ladder. She may have been correct, but I didn't get a chance to try. Every time I reached Tokyo, she backed up.

There was a structure next to the deck. The roof was about six feet below the lowest branch of the tree. I tried several things to encourage Tokyo to jump down. I brought a large two-by-four from my house. I laid it from the roof of the second structure to the rail of the deck. It looked like an easy jump for Tokyo. It was easier than jumping onto the ledge outside of Julia's window.

Tokyo was still frightened even though the dogs were nowhere in sight. Tokyo wasn't convinced that it was safe to come down from the tree.

I called Tokyo, but she would not come. My heart was broken. Even though Tokyo was not a cuddly pet, I had grown attached to her.

It was getting dark. I thought maybe she would come down from the tree when it was dark, but she did not. After more than an hour, I gave up. I did not know what to do, so I went home. I cried as I was walking into the house. I told Susan that I had failed.

We prayed together and asked for wisdom from God. I don't know why that wasn't the first thing that I did. I waited until I was desperate.

Susan suggested that we call one of our friends. Kevin and his son told us their plan.

Kevin, his son, and I went back to the large tree with my stepladder and a long thin piece of wood. I put the ladder on the deck next to the tree. I climbed the ladder like I did before. Tokyo came down the branch, but not far enough for me to grab her. Tokyo turned around and walked about six feet up the branch.

Kevin's son put the end of the stick on the branch next to Tokyo. Tokyo moved a little toward me. He continued to move the stick slowly toward Tokyo. Tokyo was more afraid of the long stick than her current situation. When Tokyo was close enough, I grabbed her.

Tokyo had a fit and started to scratch me. I held Tokyo with one hand while I held onto the ladder with the other. When I was halfway down the ladder, Kevin said, "Let go of Tokyo."

Tokyo safely landed on the deck. She jumped off the deck and ran under a bush.

We took everything back to my house and waited to see if Tokyo would follow us, but she didn't. She was still frightened, but I knew that she would not run back up the tree.

I thanked Kevin and his son for helping me, and they went home. After a couple of hours, we saw Tokyo in our yard, so we knew that she was OK even if she didn't want to come into the house right away.

Afterward, I shared my adventure with Susan. I told her that I was surprised by my emotions. I did not think that Tokyo meant that much to me.

Learning to Chop Wood

There was a fireplace in our first house when I was a child. My dad had a pile of chopped wood beneath a window. When the pile was high enough, my dad opened the window and brought the wood in. That saved him a trip outside.

I was ten years old when we moved from that house. I wasn't big enough for my dad to teach me to chop wood. The new house did not have a fireplace.

When my wife and I bought our large house, there were three fireplaces. There was a fireplace in the family room and the master bedroom. We never used the fireplace in the basement.

We bought inserts for the fireplaces in our bedroom and the family room. The heat kept us toasty warm during the cold winters.

Since we had two fireplaces, I assumed that we needed a lot of wood. I didn't know what a lot of wood was, but I bought two cords. The people who delivered the wood to our house stacked it in our breezeway.

There were a lot of trees in our backyard. We had an unending source of small twigs and branches to help start the fire.

I knew a little bit about starting fires. The wood that was delivered to us was going to be the sustaining wood. It would be necessary to take some of that wood and chop it further for the beginning of the fire.

I went to Home Depot and bought the necessary tools to chop the wood. Knowledge is primary, but not always sufficient. I had the tools, but I needed to learn the proper technique for taking large pieces of wood and making them into smaller pieces. I don't know if there's a specific word for this process, but I call it chopping wood.

Chopping wood requires practice. I did not realize how hard it was going to be.

I was not skilled in hammering nails. Chopping wood would not be any easier. I found it to be a hundred times harder. I had to hold the ax with both hands and hit the wood at just the right angle to split it. Since I was a baseball player, it was surprising that I wasn't good with the hand-to-eye in the wood-chopping process.

I learned enough to get by, but I worked hard to produce a small amount of kindling wood. I knew there must be a secret to doing it well. I needed someone who could let me in on the secret.

One of the men at our church had a wood stove in his house. He used it all winter to heat his house. If anyone knew how to chop wood, it would be him. He was a good friend, and I knew that he would be willing to help me. He wouldn't make fun of me. He would teach me no matter how long it took.

A good teacher knows his students. When he came to my house the first time, he asked me to show him what I was doing. He quickly recognized that I didn't know the difference between hardwood and softwood. I thought that wood was wood. Some burn a little faster than others, but who cares?

That was one of the reasons why I had such a hard time. I didn't care. He showed me how to quickly identify the softwood. I created a separate pile of softwood. Softwood was used for kindling wood. It was easier to chop and it burned quicker. After the fire was going, I could put any wood on that I wanted to, but he recommended using the hardwood. It burns slower and produces a good amount of heat.

I still needed to practice chopping, but I found that my task was much simpler and easier.

Fire in the Fireplace

I never want to be rushed. I hate party games that have a timer. I got upset with my children when they tried to force me to decide quickly.

Sometimes, I cause myself to rush. I often do this when I play pool. I feel like I am holding up the game if I take too long to make my shot. It sounds like I have a problem with the fear of man.

Other things caused me to rush. If it was going to rain, I tried to finish the lawn as quickly as I could. If it was dark soon, I rushed to finish my tasks outside.

The technique for starting a fire in the fireplace without filling the house with smoke is not for the fainthearted or analytical types. Once you start, you must continue. There is no time for thinking or redoing anything. You must move forward at a steady pace and instinctively know how to adjust when something unexpected happens. You can't whine and complain or blame anybody for your mess.

From the beginning of building fires in our bedroom fireplace, I felt like a pro. I can't remember a single time when there was smoke in our bedroom. I was amazed at how smoothly it went every time. I don't know if Susan was amazed, but she always encouraged me. She told me that it was fun having a fire in the fireplace in the bedroom. She liked to look at the blazing fire that slowly worked its way down to embers. They continued to produce a warm place to sit on a cold winter night as the moon was shining in the window.

When I first started building fires in the family room fireplace, I had close to the same level of success. My wife and kids cheered when I was able to build a fire with almost no smoke in just a few minutes. We enjoyed sitting around the fireplace and talking about what we would do the next day if it didn't snow.

I was my family's hero for a couple of years. Then something unexpected happened. I lost my touch, so I thought. Maybe I was too proud. Maybe I was getting old and forgot what I was supposed to do. Maybe something else happened that I didn't know about or didn't consider.

When I mentioned my dilemma to one of my friends who has a fireplace, he asked me if I cracked the window close to the fireplace before I started the fire. I told him that I did not do that because I didn't want my house to get cold before I built the fire.

Like chopping wood, I needed someone to give me the secret to building a smokeless fire. I wondered if my friend knew what he was talking about.

I told Susan that I was going to try my friend's suggestion. She said that she had no objections if I didn't have to leave the window open too long.

After I opened the window, I didn't do anything different than I did the previous time. I didn't think it was going to make a significant difference. What did I know? The answer was "nothing."

Having the window cracked open did not make building the fire in the fireplace completely flawless. Some smoke snuck into the family room as I was starting the fire, but nothing like what happened the previous time.

I decided that cracking the window was a significant part of the solution, but I still didn't know what the problem was. Could I fix the problem so that my fires would be flawless?

I went back to my friend and told him that having the window cracked open was helpful. I wanted to know why. He said that I was starving the fire at the beginning. It needed more oxygen. Once the fire is burning, it pulls oxygen from the room. Like a little sprout that's coming up out of the ground, you must baby it for a while. When I asked my friend why I started having this problem, he had no idea.

I asked another friend what I could do to help my fire get enough oxygen at the beginning. He asked me if we had installed new windows in the room where the fireplace was. We installed a lot of new windows in our house because they were drafty. That was the answer. The fledgling fire in the fireplace was able to get enough oxygen through the leaky windows but not through the new tight windows.

Opening the window while building the fire was good advice. If I knew what I was doing, I would've been able to predict the necessity of opening the window after we installed the new tight windows. I never asked anyone because I was sure that I knew what I was doing.

I was starting to see a trend, and I didn't like what I saw.

Hospitality

While I was trying to find ways to give things away, Susan was using what we had to serve others. I taught her a little, but she taught me much more.

When Susan sent me to the store, she said, "Don't waste time looking for something. If you can't find it, ask somebody."

I wondered how that was going to help. I learned that my time was just as precious as anything else that I had. The better I was using my time, the better I was showing hospitality.

I enjoyed having people in our home. Susan wanted people to enjoy being in our home.

One summer, we hosted a small church gathering on our screened-in porch. We provided fans to keep the air moving. They were passionate worshippers. They didn't stop for anything, including rainstorms. Susan baked unleavened bread for their communion services.

A woman who attended the church asked to use our porch and backyard for her girl's birthday party. Our kids were grown and were no longer living at home. The joyful sounds of the playful kids continued to echo in our minds for weeks.

On my sixtieth birthday, Susan invited two couples to celebrate with me. While we were eating dinner, worship music was playing softly in the family room. Our friends complimented Susan on her welcoming home. They could feel the presence of God's Spirit all around them.

I concluded that Susan had a special gift that I did not fully understand, but I greatly appreciated it. Susan recreated a welcoming environment in my current home. Even though Susan died a year ago, my guests continue to benefit from her gift of hospitality.

CHAPTER 15

My Job

The Interview

I enjoy being with people and I like making new friends. I like learning new things. However, enjoying and liking are very different from doing.

When I graduated from college, I put all my intellectual and emotional energy into what I believed was the best way to find and secure a career with a company. Most of the people who were close to me and whom I greatly respected followed this path. When I was hired by IBM, I believed with all my heart that I had arrived at the right location. How could anyone not like working for IBM? The company survived many financial and cultural challenges. IBM had never laid off any employees over their seventy-five years of existence. What other company could even begin to match that?

When I interviewed for a job with IBM, I was confident that it was the company that I was going to work for until I retired. I knew a lot about the company and the job that I was applying for. I was confident that I was the right person for the job. I knew that I was qualified for the job or they would not have asked me for an interview. I was told that I was interviewing the company more than they were interviewing me.

There are no guarantees in life. Not even the IBM corporation could do that for me. A few short months before Susan and I were planning to marry, the company that could do me no wrong did me wrong. I still don't know why I was laid off. I know that God was going before me and preparing the way.

For the next twenty years, I wondered where I belonged. Some companies I worked for were excellent in everything they did. However, just like IBM, they did not have enough control over everything necessary to secure their employees.

I can't say it enough times or loud enough: Susan was my greatest cheerleader. Whenever I was getting ready for an interview, she talked to me about the job and the people I would be working for. She asked a lot of good questions and gave almost no advice. She told me to trust the Lord and follow my heart. Of all the non-advice that I ever received, hers was the best.

A few times, I interviewed for a job that I knew was for me. The person who interviewed me was positive that I was right for the job and that nothing could stop me. However, I did not get the job.

A few times, I interviewed for a job and I knew almost immediately that I would not accept a position even if they offered it to me. One company seemed extremely desperate and believed that I could do a miracle for them. They wanted me to be a project manager for a group of people who were doing something that I had no knowledge of. The interviewer said that I would be reporting directly to a high-level manager who would likely implement whatever changes that I recommended. How could they promise that? After talking with Susan about the job, I gracefully refused their offer.

One day after being told that my contract was ending, I asked my manager for assistance to find another contract. The personnel representative for this large international company spent weeks sending me position descriptions that were either below my experience level or had requirements that I couldn't fake.

I called Dawn on the phone. She helped me find some of my previous positions. She was the one who connected me with my current employer. When I told her that things were not going as well as I hoped, she was distressed. She wasn't just a typical headhunter.

She cared for her clients and was my friend. I often called her even when I didn't need any assistance. We had fun conversations. She said that I could call her whenever I wanted to. One afternoon, I called her as she was on her way to get married. Someone in the limo said, "Don't answer your phone." Dawn responded, "I must, it's Rich Payne."

I told Dawn that I was looking for a job and my current employer was not able to find anything reasonable.

Dawn said, "Come work for me."

I wondered what that meant. I knew that she was sincere. She wouldn't joke about something like that, but I couldn't imagine how I could help her. I couldn't find a job for myself. My mind wandered into the area of administration, but I did not want to assume anything.

I asked, "What kind of a job could you see me doing for you?"

She said, "I'm sure I can find a job for you. Something like what you've been doing for the last few years."

I was still confused. She didn't say she would find me a job. She said she wanted me to work for her. I said, "I'm confused. I trust you, but help me understand what you're offering."

She chuckled, "I forgot to tell you. Rich, I started my own company. You said that I was so good at finding jobs for other people, that I should have my own company."

I said, "Are you asking me to work for your new company?"

She said, "I need people like you in my company. I only have a few employees. Does that make you uncomfortable?"

I responded, "Over the years, you have been so good at finding me a job. If I work directly for you, I'm sure you'll do even a better job of finding me positions that match my experience and interest."

She said, "I want you to talk to Mark. I think you worked with him in the past."

The name sounded familiar to me, but I couldn't remember exactly what we did together. I wondered if he remembered more about me than I remembered about him. I hoped so because he was going to be hiring me.

I talked to Mark on the phone. He reminded me of the project that we worked on together. It was a large contract and he did not work in my group. I must've had a good reputation for him to remember me.

Mark told me that there was an open position in his contract and that I would be the right person for the job. There was no question in his mind that I would be the kind of employee that they needed in their fledging company.

I asked Mark if he was going to be in the interview the next morning. He said that he would meet me in the lobby, but he could not be in the interview. The prime company had to interview me independently. Dawn's company was a subcontractor. This was common. I told Mark that I was up for the challenge, so he set up the interview.

The next morning, I met Mark in the lobby. I knew that it was Mark even though I did not remember what he looked like. He was looking for me. It was easy because I was the only one coming for an interview.

When I sat in the conference room for the interview, several of the members of the team welcomed me. It was a low-key conversation. It seemed like they wanted to finish the interview so that they could hire me. I could see myself working for these people, but the manager wasn't there. The manager had to at least show up for the interview. That's what I thought. They apologized for him not being there. They said that he would arrive shortly.

When the manager arrived, he apologized for being late. I graciously accepted his apology.

The manager had an unopened bag of candy. He tossed it onto the conference room table. He asked, "Rich, would you like a piece of candy?"

I had never been to an interview where the hiring manager asked me if I wanted a piece of candy, but there was nothing wrong with that. Everybody eats candy. He figured I must too.

I responded graciously, "Thank you for the offering. I would like a piece of candy; however, I want to wait until the interview is completed. I don't want to be distracted by eating candy."

The manager said, "I like that answer. It is not required for you to bring or eat snacks on this project; however, you must be ready when they are brought in. Everyone does their own thing."

After the interview, I ate a piece of candy.

I talked to Mark and told him that I would fit in. He said that he was pleased. He knew that I would enjoy working on his project. He said that we would have an opportunity to talk more in the next few days.

I enjoyed working on that project with Mark. It had its normal set of challenges, but overall, it was a great place to work.

I worked for Dawn and Mark's company until I retired. The company has continued to grow and flourish. I am not surprised. It was a wonderful company to work for.

Calling Home

As soon as I said, "I do," I wanted to be with my wife continuously. Some people thought that was unrealistic, and it probably was. But what's wrong with wanting it?

When we married, Susan was still working in a regular job. She was planning to quit working as soon as we had children. We didn't condemn other couples for making a different decision; however, this is what we believed was the best for our children. As soon as we made the decision to adopt children, we believed that it was even more important that the kids know who their parents are.

A few months prior to our wedding, I was looking for a job because I was laid off in the summer. Frequently, I visited Susan at her office. She was an administrative assistant. Her boss was OK with me coming by as long as I didn't keep Susan from doing your job.

When I started my new job, the location was in northern Virginia. I had a long drive during rush hour from Gaithersburg. I got up early in the morning to try to avoid some of the morning rush. My flexible schedule allowed me to leave early so that I could avoid some of the afternoon rush. I could not avoid all the rush hour. There were a lot of cars on the road all the time.

I only had one reasonable way to get to work. I took the Washington Beltway. Anytime there was a slowdown, it would take me close to two hours to get home. Cell phones were just becoming common. I got an inexpensive phone through my company. The first fifteen minutes each month were free. After that, I had to pay a big fee. I put the cell phone in the glove compartment of my car. I only used it if I had to call Susan on the way home from work.

Emotionally, I was a totally different person after I got married. I was able to live a somewhat normal life, but my desire was always to be with my wife. Some people didn't understand.

My routine was to call my wife on my lunch break. Sometimes, that was 11:00 a.m. Sometimes, it was much later. I often brought my lunch so that I could sit at my desk and talk to my wife while I was eating. She might be eating at the same time. I imagined I was eating with her.

One of my coworkers asked me why my daughter always answered the phone whenever I called home. I love my daughter, and she loves me. I'm not saying she refused to answer the telephone, but she didn't answer on a regular basis. When I called home, my daughter was usually at school.

I asked my coworker, "Why do you think my daughter answers the phone when I call home?"

He said, "When you greet the person who answers the phone, you always call her sweetie."

I said, "My wife always answers the phone. She is my sweetie."

My coworker didn't comment, but I knew what he was thinking. He probably never called his wife sweetie.

I wasn't going to deny who I was. I wasn't going to act the way my coworkers wanted me to act. It was difficult working in an environment like that. No one outwardly criticized or made fun of

115

me because I loved my wife and called her sweetie. I just sensed that I was different from my coworkers.

I loved to talk to my bird on the phone. It was Susan's bird, which I adopted when we married. That was a challenge all by itself. I never had a bird for a pet. You can't treat a bird like you can a dog or a cat. I knew what I couldn't do, but it was hard for me to figure out what I was supposed to do.

Before we married, Susan's bird talked to me on the phone. After we married, why would that change? I talked to my bird more. My coworkers had more to think about me. We had a cockatiel. They have wonderful personalities and they love to mimic everything, including human voices.

Our cockatiel was confused. Winsome recognized my voice and thought that I was inside the telephone. He would say "hello." Sometimes, he started singing a song. When he wanted me to come home right away, he knocked on the telephone with his beak. He expected me to open the phone and jump out. I tried telling these stories to my coworkers, but they didn't think they were funny or interesting.

Why would I care what my coworkers thought of my interaction with my family and my bird? Why would I feel like I needed to explain?

I wanted to fit in. If my coworkers liked to go out for lunch, I wanted to go with them. If my coworkers had a bowling league at lunchtime, I wanted to bowl with them. I didn't think it was necessary to do everything that everybody wanted to do, but I wanted to do some things with them. I didn't want to be like a robot at work. I wanted to show some of my personality and interests. We were all different, but I didn't want to be *too different*.

On Friday afternoons when the managers and team leaders all left, some of the rowdier members of my project called across the room to each other. Sometimes, it was just fun. Other times, they got out of hand.

My desk was on the side of the room with several jokesters that regularly stayed late on Friday. On the other side of the room, where the managers sat, was just one person.

He said something that was offensive to me. I knew he wasn't directing it to me but to the ones sitting close to me.

Each night when I arrived, Susan asked me how my day was. She knew what I wanted to say, but it was OK if I didn't. She loved me just the same.

Top Honors

I never thought that life was fair. If it was, I would not have received most of the good things. I didn't deserve them.

There were also things that I probably should have received credit for, but I did not. These are the things that trip me up. These are the things that leave me scared. These are the things that lock me in dungeons and keep me from feeling free to continue with what I know I should be doing.

Emotional locks can be just as tricky as physical locks. Sometimes, I was given the combination to a lock and I still could not open it. I was told that it required a special touch. The people who had been on the project for years could open the combination locks for the filing cabinets. I struggled so much that I often gave up. If I needed to get access to one of the file drawers, I waited until someone was available to open it for me.

The life of a software engineer is exciting. I was more than a computer programmer. That was fun and challenging enough, but managers don't want employees who can do only one thing. As new opportunities arise, a good manager will assign a task to someone who has never done it before. It was fun to learn to do new things. Because technology was changing so fast, most software engineers considered themselves in school continuously.

As well as being technically proficient, I branched out into other areas. Because I enjoyed standing in front of people and giving reports, my manager trained me to become a team leader. Because

I had strong organizational skills, I was given an opportunity to become a project manager.

The management of one of my projects was reorganized. My new manager wanted to maximize the skills of the employees.

I was the lead software engineer on the project. I was given a complex task to convert a program that was not well written so that it could be easily maintained. My coworkers applauded me for finishing the task quickly.

When the new manager was evaluating her senior-level employees, she realized that one employee would only fit the position of a lead software engineer. She put him in that position even though he was recently added to the team. The second senior-level employee had experience being a team leader, so the manager made that assignment.

I was the third senior-level person. When the manager discussed her staffing assignments with me, she said that it was clear to her that I was qualified to fill all three of the senior-level positions. However, I was the only one who had experience as a project manager. I told the manager that I would prefer to continue in the software lead position; however, I understood why she made the decision that she did. I joyfully accepted the assignment that she gave me.

When our project was completed, corporate management decided to give an award for technical achievement. The award was given to a single individual. Even though I was the one who successfully created a program that could be maintained, I was not given the award. The award was given to the person who was the current technical lead.

At the ceremony, I was disappointed. My coworkers who had been on the project for a significant period quietly voiced their disapproval of the decision to give the award to the newcomer instead of me. They said that I deserved the award. The vote of confidence from my coworkers was greater than any amount of money. The success of the team is more important than the success of any member.

CHAPTER 16

My Mate

The Countryside

When I want to relax, I sit outside. The singing birds remind me to rejoice in the presence of the Lord. I close my eyes and feel the gentle breeze. The gentle voice of the Lord draws me into His presence.

Some of my friends don't understand. They love me anyway. When I met Susan, I knew that she was different. When she didn't understand something about me, she wanted me to help her understand. I wondered why, but I didn't ask. I rarely asked anything. Susan told me that it was OK to ask. It wasn't the asking but how you asked. Susan knew how to ask. She never made me uncomfortable.

After we married, I learned a lot, and I wished I had enough courage to ask her sooner. I was amazed that so few people knew the real Susan. I felt that God hid things from me so that I would enjoy discovering her precious heart.

Susan enjoyed nature as much as I did. A fun afternoon was taking Susan on a drive through the countryside. Our destination was secondary. She always had a wonderful suggestion for a fun trip, but we always enjoyed the beautiful scenes along the way.

Susan and I loved the fall. September was a perfect month to get married. October was a perfect month to see the beautiful leaves before they fell off the trees. Even sitting on our back porch gave us great delight. We didn't try hard, but it seemed like we found houses that had a beautiful view from our back porch.

Even with our daily views of nature, Susan and I still treasured the times when we could drive through the countryside and the mountains.

Our Anniversaries

When Susan and I returned from our honeymoon, we didn't want to wait a year for an anniversary celebration. We celebrated on the eleventh of each month. We took turns planning our celebrations.

As soon as one month's anniversary celebration was over, we started planning for the next one. When it was Susan's turn, I tried to imagine what she would do to surprise me. She was better at coming up with a surprise than I was. She came from a family that was always having a party.

After one year of celebrating every month, we switched to having our celebrations annually. I don't remember why we made that decision. We may have run out of new things to do. However, our yearly celebrations were still exciting. Some were simple, like going out to dinner at a special restaurant. Others took a lot of planning and money.

We played the memory game. During each of our anniversary celebrations, we tried to recall what we did for each of the previous ones. For the first few years, it was easy. Some of the less memorable ones from many years before faded from our memory. I enjoyed reminiscing with my precious wife, even though I wasn't good at remembering. Some people take pictures of every fun activity, but Susan and I did not. Even though our phones had limited memory, we could've taken one picture on each of our anniversaries, but sadly, we did not.

Susan and I were married for thirty years. I did not expect to remember every anniversary or even half of them. I wondered if I would have to carefully select the anniversaries to include in this chapter. That didn't happen because I remembered so few.

We enjoyed the gardens. The fall was a beautiful time of the year, so we frequently searched for gardens to walk through. Longwood Gardens is close to my hometown. It was a favorite place for our family to bring out-of-town guests.

We stayed in a B&B close to Longwood Gardens for one of our earlier anniversaries. They had an amazing light show every evening. It gave the impression of fireworks as the colored lights lit up the waterworks. When I played the video, it was hard for me to believe that there was no sound. I would not have believed it if I hadn't been there.

Susan and I loved German food. There was a German restaurant a few miles away from our house. We ate there when they had live music. It was a good restaurant, and there were few German restaurants in our area. We wondered why it wasn't more popular. When the restaurant closed, we did not mind driving farther for good German food.

The Bavarian Inn and Restaurant overlooks the Potomac River in Shepherdstown. I took Susan there several times for dinner. For one of our anniversary celebrations, we stayed at the inn. Our balcony overlooked the river. As we sat in the cool evening, we noticed a bright light in the sky. It was too far to distinguish what it was. Since the light was not moving, we agreed that it was not an airplane or a helicopter. If it were a geosynchronous satellite, it would be in an unusually low orbit.

On the morning of September 11, 2001, I was sitting at my desk wondering why I had to be so far away from my precious wife on our eighth anniversary. We were going out for our special dinner later in the week, but we were still going to celebrate our anniversary at home that evening.

As I stared at my computer screen, lacking motivation, one of my coworkers announced that a commercial airliner hit one of the twin towers in New York City. He was always joking around like that. No one took him seriously. After about twenty minutes, he told us with a serious look on his face that a second airplane hit the second tower. We couldn't believe that this was a joke. How could he say such a thing?

Another employee checked the Internet for emergency messages. He was able to confirm that both towers had been hit. The initial report was that both airplanes were commercial airliners. It was more than I could handle. The first thing that went through my mind was, "Are we safe?" Then my heart went out to my family.

Shortly after this report, our supervisor told us that there would be an announcement soon. We would all be asked to leave the facility immediately. Our supervisor gave us permission to leave before the announcement was made so that we would have an opportunity to leave the parking lot before the mass exit. I found out later that some people sat in the parking lot for several hours.

As soon as I was safely out of the parking lot, I tried to call my wife. All the cell phone connections were already in use. I knew that my wife was going to be concerned for me. I was no longer concerned about my safety. I wanted my wife to have peace in her heart, but I couldn't talk to her.

When I arrived, my wife was overjoyed to see me. She asked me if I knew what was happening. I told her that it would probably be a few days before the whole story would be known.

We were planning to have our special anniversary dinner at a Middle Eastern restaurant in downtown Washington, DC, in a few days. We changed our plans so that we would be closer to home. We also did not want to be somewhere that might be racially charged.

Susan loved to research about our ancestors. My dad gave her the information that he had. Except for one Cherokee Indian woman, all my ancestors were from Scotland. Most of Susan's ancestors were from Ireland.

We traveled to Scotland and Ireland in 2018. Susan created an itinerary that took us to several towns where our ancestors were born. I learned to drive on the left side of the road. The first few days were stressful, but then I started to feel more comfortable.

As we visited cemeteries, Susan looked for members of our family tree. We stopped at a pub in Ireland. Susan asked the owner if he knew anyone who lived nearby with the same last name as her ancestor. Susan talked to a local man on the phone. Seeing the smile on Susan's face was worth the effort.

My greatest joy from this anniversary trip was staying in the castle that one of my ancestors owned. The curtains and the bedspread were made from the tartan for my clan.

Dance

When I was growing up, I was advised to avoid certain things. One that is often criticized is abstinence from dancing. Like drinking alcohol, I do not believe that there is anything intrinsically wrong with dancing. Dancing is a good form of exercise and can be artistic.

The people who advise against dancing are concerned that dancing can lead to inappropriate thoughts about and actions toward your partner. I choose to avoid dancing if I can. I do not judge others for making a different decision; however, I know that it is the best for me.

For one of our anniversary celebrations, Susan and I ate dinner on a boat called the *Dandy*. There was a dance floor and Susan asked me if I would dance with her. Susan was the only person that I would consider dancing with. She knew how I felt about dancing. I had no experience dancing, but she wanted to dance with me anyway. How could I say no?

I watched other people dance, and I had a general idea of what was expected of the man. As we were dancing, I looked into Susan's eyes. She had the look that I had seen many times before. It was the look that said, "You don't have to impress me or anybody else. I love you just the way you are."

When we sat down, Susan said to me, "I enjoy dancing with you. You may not believe me, but you are a good dancer."

Sacrifice of Love

I keep looking at the title of this book and wonder if there was anything in my relationship with Susan that could be classified as a lock.

There's no way that I could write an autobiography and not include many things that Susan and I did together and what she meant to me. She lived with me for half of my life. I cannot say that about anybody else.

Before I married Susan, I believed that I did a lot of things out of sacrificial love. I also did a lot of things that were self-preservation. Some things I did were just selfish.

I can't summarize my thirty years with Susan in a few pages or even a few hundred pages. As I remember things, I write about them. In several places, I touch on things that are indications of sacrificial love. I don't want to sound proud, but since I loved my wife dearly, I'm not surprised that I can think of things that I did that were sacrificial love.

Susan was my best cheerleader. Get used to reading it because it was so true and so rare. I know many couples that did not have the relationship that I had with Susan. There's no question that she was gifted, but she would often sacrifice a lot for me. She sacrificed for a lot of other people too.

Susan struggled a lot with her physical health. I was glad that I had a flexible work schedule so that I could be with Susan when she needed me.

When Susan had open-heart surgery, she was transferred to a hospital that was about forty-five minutes driving time from our house. If the traffic was bad, the trip took much longer. I took time off to be with Susan, but the drive back and forth was too much for me.

The surgery went well. Susan was well cared for at the hospital. I knew that she would recover quickly even if I was just there during normal visiting hours. There wasn't much for me to do, but I wanted to be there. So I was.

Most hospitals do not have a place for a relative to sleep overnight. The insurance company pays for care for the patient but not the family. That wasn't good enough for me. The staff told me that I did not have to leave at any time. If I wanted to stay overnight, it was OK, but I had to figure things out for myself.

There was a nice waiting area close to Susan's room. It was comfortable to sit, but there was no provision for someone who wanted to sleep other than sitting up. If I sat in a chair in the middle of the night, I might doze off for a short time, but I would not get any reasonable amount of sleep. I didn't care. If they were going to let me stay there, then I was going to stay.

The first two nights, I slept on a couch in the waiting area. It was not comfortable, but it was better than sitting up.

God had mercy on me. The staff transferred Susan to another room on the same floor. The room was the only room that had extra space for family members to sleep. Inside the room was an area with a pullout bed. They gave me two pillows and a blanket. It wasn't some of my best sleep, but it was much better than sleeping on the couch in the waiting area.

Working with insurance companies is a heartache. The rehabilitation center did not know if Medicare or my private insurance for Susan was primary. They could not receive Susan until the insurance was straightened out. I was working for Dawn. Even though she was on vacation, she helped me make the arrangements for my wife's care. Medicare has complicated rules for small companies. The hospital understood how to submit the medical forms. I did not understand why the rehabilitation center was confused. With Dawn's help, the insurance was arranged.

CHAPTER 17

Keeping the Vision

Realignment

Everyone is willing to give up something of value to help a person or for a cause. Giving my time to the ones I love is not a sacrifice. I enjoy helping someone move or entertaining a young boy while his mother runs errands.

Susan and I hosted Bible studies and prayer meetings. We continued to help with the children's ministry at our church even after our kids were grown. Susan was a great cook and loved to prepare meals for new mothers and sick friends.

God calls us to dream with Him. He puts desires in our hearts and then He shows us the vision. The vision may be the same, even though individual desires are different.

Susan and I were ready to give up what we had to see a greater harvest in the future. We knew that the vision would require major changes.

There were things from my past that I knew would be hindrances if I did not learn to deal with them. When the time came to make difficult decisions, would I be ready? When God asked me to step out into the unknown, would I hesitate? When other people's desires did not align with mine, would I have the courage to look for the realignment?

If I reached some of my goals, would I be satisfied or would I continue to pursue everything within the vision?

Our large home, which I once called a retreat center, became more than I could manage. Our kids were grown and moved away. Our beautiful pool was not being used but required a significant amount of my time and money to maintain. We rarely used our fireplaces. I did not have the time or the energy to take care of our lawn and shrubs.

It was time for us to downsize, but we weren't sure what that meant. I was close to retirement, but not retired. We looked at several places nearby, but none seemed right. We didn't want to spend money on things that would give us little benefit.

The Move to Frederick

God speaks in different ways. He gives us choices, but when our hearts are to follow Him, He gives us desires to move along the path that He prepared for us. We must listen carefully to what He is saying. He doesn't promise that things will be easy, but He does promise that He will be with us.

Susan and I assumed that God wanted us to stay in the Gaithersburg area. We searched for retirement homes and smaller houses that might meet our needs. We didn't know what our needs would be in five or ten years. We wondered if we should prepare for when we would need more medical assistance.

I could see us still living in Gaithersburg, but moving to another area was still in consideration. The vision for our church was to reach our neighboring communities as well as Gaithersburg. The leaders were considering several towns, including Frederick.

Frederick is twenty-five miles north of Gaithersburg. It was considered far enough that we could have a meeting there as well as in Gaithersburg. While Susan and I were looking for a new place to live, our church had not decided about Frederick.

The Lord put a desire in our hearts for the people of Frederick.

We found an easy-to-manage home a few miles outside of Frederick in the town of New Market. Susan loved visiting New Market when she was single, and she dreamed of living there. Sometimes, the Lord does that. You have a desire to go someplace or do something, but you're not sure why.

In the same week that we put an offer on our house, our church announced that they would have a meeting in Frederick.

Buying a house and moving during the pandemic was not easy. Finding a place to have a church meeting was a greater challenge. We knew that the Lord was doing something, and we were ready to do it with Him.

Continuing Through Hardships

No new adventure is easy but always exciting. Sometimes, when I was asked to step out of the boat, it seemed impossible even when there were no waves. When the trials came, I quickly forgot how impossible the task originally seemed.

Susan and I were able to buy our new house before we sold the old house. Loans and mortgages can be a challenge, but they are also a great blessing when things work for you. We were able to make changes to our new house and move stress-free.

Because it was still in the middle of the pandemic, there were few houses on the market. Lots of people looked at our house. Our real estate agent said that he had never had so many showings of a house in such a short period. There were lots of people who viewed the house, but we were wondering when we would receive an offer. When it finally came, I was glad to be released from that responsibility.

While we were working through our challenges, we joined the pioneers from our church as they began their adventure in Frederick.

The excitement of seeing local people joining our young fellowship and engaging people in the local parks was often interrupted by Susan's frequent trips to the hospital. I received an amazing amount of support from our friends who attended both meetings. Many new members from Frederick also prayed for my wife and me.

Some of our young adult friends accepted our invitation to pray with us in our home. When Susan was not able to attend our church meetings, the meetings in our home encouraged Susan. She also received frequent visits when she was in the hospital and rehabilitation centers. Her visitors often said that they were encouraged by Susan.

In addition to the ministries and activities of our church, Susan and I had a desire to pray for the children in our local schools. We took our prayer list and parked in a school parking lot at lunchtime. As we observed the children sitting outside the school building, we were led by the Spirit as we interceded for them. We longed to go inside the building and talk to the students individually, but we knew that that was for another time.

We often saw a student sitting alone. I desperately wanted to know his story. How was he hurting? Had he given up on life? Would he respond if someone showed him love? What kind of dungeon was he locked in? Did I know something that I could share with him to set him free? If so, how would I do it?

Retirement

We lived in a fifty-five-plus community close to Frederick. Each home must have one resident who is fifty-five years or older. Most of the people in our community are retired. Many are still active, and they organize events. The man who lives two doors down is active and frequently invites me to join in.

One Friday morning as I was leaving for work, my neighbor was preparing to go on a bike ride. He called out to me, "Rich, we go on a bike ride every Friday morning. Would you like to go with us?"

I said, "I haven't ridden a bike in a long time, and I don't think I have time. I must go to work."

In his friendly voice, he said, "You need to retire. You are in a retirement community."

I responded, "I will give that some consideration."

Another day, my neighborhood friend asked me if I would like to play golf. I told him that I had not played in a long time and I did not have golf clubs. He said that I could borrow some of his.

When I went for a physical, the nurse told me that I needed more exercise. She asked me for my plan. I told her I would start walking every day if I could. She instructed me to work up to a twenty-minute walk each day. I could see walking twenty minutes a day, but maybe not every day.

The men in our Frederick church planned outreach activities. They scheduled a dinner at a local bar. I said I wasn't interested in going to a bar. They said I didn't have to drink alcohol. I could just eat with them and find people to talk to.

Reluctantly, I agreed to go. I stopped at our house before I went to dinner. Susan was relaxing after chopping the vegetables for her dinner. When I asked her how she was doing, I was surprised at her response.

She said, "I don't feel well."

Susan was usually articulate. She had no problem telling me how she was feeling and whether she needed me to stay with her.

I said, "I should stay home with you tonight. Tell me more about how you are feeling. What can I do for you?"

She said sternly, "I already told you that I don't feel well."

I knew that I needed help. I told Susan that I was going to call 911 and get some help. She just stared at me. Susan was not herself.

After Susan was treated at the hospital and we followed up with her doctor, I realized that I could not continue to work full-time. I had a flexible work schedule, but I could not continue taking as much time as I needed to care for her.

I loved my wife, and I loved caring for her. I was willing to give up anything for her. Until this point, I thought carefully before I made a major decision. Susan and I usually made decisions together, but I wasn't sure how I was going to decide to retire.

Susan and I prayed together. She believed that I would hear from the Lord. This was the first time that Susan wanted to help me talk through a decision, but we both realized that she wasn't able to.

Within a few weeks, I retired. I never regretted my decision. Susan needed me, and I was more available to care for her.

Susan Never Stopped Helping Me

A year and a half later, Susan was in a rehabilitation center after a stroke. She asked me when she could go home. I said the staff was planning an evaluation next week. I took Susan in a wheelchair to the gift shop. We selected a wreath to hang on our front door. I hung the wreath with the expectation that she would enjoy seeing it when she returned home.

On the next Saturday, I planned to go to a prophetic meeting but I changed my mind. When I told Susan that I was going to stay with her, she said, "You must go. I can't hold you back."

Even in her weakened state, Susan continued to encourage me to pursue the vision. That was the last time that Susan helped me make a difficult decision.

Instead of going home, a few days later, she returned to the hospital. I watched as her condition deteriorated over the next week.

As they were taking Susan to the ICU, the doctor was trying to get her to answer questions about her care. Susan said, "My husband will make all the decisions for me." I am confident that the decisions I made while she was in the ICU were consistent with her desires.

The evening Susan went home to be with her Lord, there was an incredibly beautiful sunset. One of our pastors sent me a note saying that he thought it was God welcoming a saint into heaven.

PART V

Alone Again

CHAPTER 18

The Right Stuff

Slowing Down

I like fun surprises. I don't get enough in my life, so I create them for myself. I have a set of pictures on my computer, my phone, and my watch. A picture is selected at random for each device. It is fun because I don't know which picture will be displayed.

As I looked out the window, I could see that the shadow of my house was covering my backyard. A few minutes later, the shadow had extended into the farm behind my house.

I wasn't planning to write today. These two images came to my mind, and I realized how they were connected.

The pictures keep me from forgetting the wonderful things that God has given me. My life today consists of sixty-five years of life-giving experiences. I only want to remember the fun things, but my struggles today are caused by unresolved issues from my past. The light of my former life casts an evergrowing shadow that seems to be consuming the vision that God gave me.

I am surprised that I am no longer writing about my past. I'm writing about my life today. My slowing down began a few years ago. I accept the fact that my body is slowing down, but I know that I can be reenergized for the things in my book that are left to be accomplished.

This is the first October that I am experiencing without my wife. I celebrated her life by going to a farm on the one-year anniversary of the day she died and went to be with her Lord. I remembered an experience we had together. Today, I watched children play, which reminds me of the new life I have in Christ.

As I watched the children, I was reminded once again of the simpler things of life.

Now What?

It is a time of transition, but I'm not sure how long it will be. I need to be around people who can help me, not people who are trying to fix me.

I was feeling the same just before I got married. Now, some things are different, but other things are still the same.

Am I really alone? Why do I still have to ask this question?

When I was single, I often felt that I was alone, even though I knew God was with me. He never left me alone.

Until recently, I wondered if Jesus knows what it is like to feel alone. It is easy to find answers to this kind of question. If I want to know how Jesus feels, I ask Him.

Jesus answered, "There are two kinds of feeling alone. When I was in the garden, I wanted my closest friends to be with me, but they were not.

"My physical feeling alone was in anticipation of my spiritual feeling alone. Your physical feeling alone can be comforted. Because I suffered through being alone from Heavenly Father, you do not have to."

After Susan died, I asked Jesus many times, "Why am I still here?"

His answer was always the same: "I still have things I want you to do for my Kingdom. Do you remember the vision? Do you remember the dream? The dream did not die with Susan."

I asked, "How can I continue the dream without Susan?"

There is always a short answer that Jesus asks me to accept even though I don't understand how it can happen. When my heart is ready, He begins to reveal the details of His plan.

A Different Shape

In my book *Soul Survivors*, I share the story of Susan losing her wedding ring. For most women, her wedding ring is her most cherished possession. It reminds her of the devotion her husband has toward her.

Before I asked Susan to marry me, I wondered if I should buy a ring for her or ask her to go with me to help select the engagement ring. I asked my dad to help me make the decision. He said that I would know in my heart.

I believed Susan would be OK with the decision either way, but if given a choice, she would prefer to go with me to pick out her ring. When I asked her to marry me, I did not have a ring in my hand. Susan told me that I was correct. I could not have made a mistake, but she preferred to help select her ring.

After we married, the ring fell off her hand and was crushed by a car. The gold and the diamonds of the original ring were used to design a new ring. It did not look like the original ring. Even though it was in a different shape, it still represented my love for her.

The Lord said to me, "I want you to continue with what is in your heart. I did not remove it from your heart because I don't want you to give up on it. It may not look the same to those close to you, but it is the same dream. The dream that is in your heart is no less significant now. Just like the new ring, the dream will appear to some to be a different shape."

Identifying the Locks

God has a book that contains the things that He wants me to do in my life. He loves to dream, and He wants somebody to dream with.

I have free will, so I may not do everything He wants me to do. However, my desire is to continue with each of the dreams that God shares with me.

During this time of uncertainty, after the loss of my wife, I appreciate the many things that God provides to help me deal with the emotions and challenges that are coming at me each day.

Even when I know what God wants me to do, I hesitate. How can I become totally free?

It is hurricane season. The clouds cause dark nights. Down south, there are hurricanes that are devastating large areas. We're just getting the remnants.

That's the way I feel. I can't point to anything specific. I lack energy and excitement in my life, but I don't know why.

This is where I am and this is what I do, but where do I belong? My life today can be characterized by everything that I have experienced. I will be a different person tomorrow.

I do not have to continue to be locked in the dungeon that I was mercilessly thrown into.

I can adjust my living conditions and my physical health. Most people pursue these and have some level of success.

My failures today are linked to things in my past that I am unaware of. How can I change something when I don't know how to explain what it is? How do I escape through a door that I cannot find?

If I live each day in ignorance of my past, I do myself a great injustice. I have the potential for so much more.

I am looking for keys that can unlock doors that I have been trying to open. It is easier to remove a lock from an open door.

My wife, Susan, was continually an inspiration to me. Almost effortlessly, she was able to identify her limitations and how to overcome them. Even now, I can learn from her.

Susan was in a hospital bed, all connected and not feeling well. She did not know how long she was going to be there. She did not allow her limitations to keep her from doing what she needed to do. She told me what gift to send to her young nephew. I have a video of Susan doing a FaceTime with her young nephew when he received the gift.

Send Help

I realized that God had been preparing me for this season. I have always enjoyed writing. I have always enjoyed talking to and encouraging children. It is not surprising, at least it should not be, that God wants me to write children's stories. I never thought about it until a couple of years ago.

I decided to retire early when I wanted to be more available for my wife. Susan was in and out of the hospital often during the previous several years, but it got to the point where I couldn't be with her as much as I wanted to. I was always playing catchup with my job.

After I retired, my wife and I were talking about what God wanted me to do. My highest priority was to care for my wife. When I was working, Susan wasn't in the hospital or a rehab center all the time. She was at home by herself when I was working. Now that I was at home, I had a time when I could be doing other things while caring for her.

One morning, I had an impression of going to a bookstore. I believed that God's Spirit was guiding me. Susan said that she would be fine while I was away for a few hours.

I walked around the bookstore for almost an hour. I bought an interesting book that was not expensive. I do not like spending money on myself. The book has ideas for people who have writer's block.

I enjoyed working through the book. When I saw the suggestion to write a short children's story where the prevalent letter is L, I was intrigued.

After I wrote a story, I showed it to Susan. She said that it was good, and she thought that children would enjoy it. I continued to go through the book of suggestions. Some of the ideas were boring, but others were interesting.

After about a month, I went back to the suggestion of writing children's stories. I wrote one more. Then Susan was continually sick over an extended period. I only wrote a few more children's stories.

Susan died in early October 2023. For the next few weeks, I wasn't coming up with anything creative.

By the end of the year, I realized that the stories I had been writing over the past year and a half were preparing me for what God wanted me to do after Susan died. The practice of writing the children's stories helped for what God wants me to do now. I also found that the content of the stories was helpful for my life. God led me to write stories that I would need to reread after Susan died.

I enjoyed writing the children's stories. Amazingly, I enjoy reading them even more.

I must be careful to not eliminate good things that are happening in my life just because I don't know why or how. Much of what I expected to happen is being replaced with things that are much better for me.

When I first moved out on my own, it took me at least a year before I was comfortable allowing myself to be myself. I was not trying to hide my faults. I was protecting myself from feeling like I had nothing to contribute. I don't need to do that anymore.

My perception was that I was confused. Sometimes, perception is more important to the struggling person than reality is.

I have a small understanding of the ability of God to help His children in their time of need. I thought I was only writing the stories for children, but the Lord was also teaching me at the same time.

Friends Who Stay Up with Me

What is a friend? Don't ask Facebook. They want you to be friends with people who you have nothing in common with. You can be a friend of a friend. You can be a friend if you went to the same university. You can be a friend if you have a common interest. You can be a friend if you live in the same town. Some people have thousands of Facebook friends.

Don't confuse a friend with an acquaintance. There are lots of nice people in your life. You like the guy next door because he has a cute dog that's friendly. You like the person who cuts your hair. Some people like their instructors in school. If you're sick, some of these people will help you out by bringing you dinner. If you're hurt, they might take you to the hospital. They might even loan you money. Make sure that you have an opportunity to pay them back.

What is a friend? You can have friends that you talk to and make you feel good.

All these people are nice people. I want to have them around me. I don't want to be alone if I have a problem or a need.

What if your friend doesn't understand you? What if your friend thinks you're different? What if your friend thinks he knows how to solve your problems, but you don't think he's helpful?

What happens when you disappoint your friend? Does your friend get upset with you? Does your friend decide that he's going to unfriend you? Does your friend tell all your other friends that they need to stop helping you?

What if you're struggling with something that becomes burdensome to your friend? If he says you're on your own, was he ever a friend?

Does your friend have to like what you do or be like you?

Is your friend someone that makes you like your enemies more?

Why does it matter anyway?

People who pretend to be your friends are the ones who throw you into a dungeon, lock the door, and throw away the key. I knew people like that. I tried to be their friend. Every time I took one step forward, they pushed me back two.

I have never been able to live my life by myself. I always need people. Sometimes, I tried too hard to be a friend. Sometimes, I tried too hard to make people like me.

A true friend is like a good locksmith. When you call him, he doesn't ask you what your problem is before he comes. If he doesn't have a clue about how to help you, he doesn't say that you are on your own. Together, you work out the solution.

A true friend reminds you that "you plus God" is always a majority. A true friend reminds you that your past failures do not define you. A true friend rejoices when you rejoice and mourns when you mourn. A true friend cares for you even when he has no idea how to care for you. He asks God for wisdom, and he receives it. A true friend gives up his life for you.

A good friend desires to be a true friend but often comes up short. A good friend has compassion for you when you are locked. A good friend looks like a locksmith who can unlock your door and remove the lock.

I've had good friends, and I've always desired to be a good friend. Sometimes, I demand too much of my friends and push them away. Sometimes, my friends seem to demand too much of me. I want to remain true to my friends, but sometimes I fail.

When I fail, I feel like I have been thrown into a dungeon. I must decide. Will I stay there long enough to allow the door to be locked or will I climb out? Will somebody be there to throw me a rope?

I realized that I had a true friend when I was seven years old. I did not see Him standing next to me, but He was there. I wanted to see and hear Him.

I asked Jesus how to be a good friend. I was amazed that I heard an answer. He told me that I was already a good friend. The next step was to learn to be a true friend. Sometimes, Jesus doesn't speak the way we speak, but when I listen, I always hear Him.

I was learning to read. I read the Bible, but I didn't understand much. My parents and teachers at church explained things to me in little children's ways. I memorized Psalm 100 in the King James Version. It says to make a joyful noise. I can make a noise that is joyful. The Bible says to do it in a way that shares my heart with God and those around me.

I realized that Jesus was not only a good friend but also a true friend. I desired to be like Jesus. I guessed it would take me a long time, maybe a year or two. I was wrong. I can never become a true friend, but I am becoming a true friend.

CHAPTER 19

The Promise

The Reoccurring Dream

When my wife and I moved to our new house, we struggled as we sold and gave away things that were precious to us. We could not keep everything, and the greatest challenge was books. We had bookshelves everywhere. We thought that we would never get through the books in the basement.

Most of the books we keep are now on a few bookshelves in our loft that we made into a study. One morning, I was looking for a reminder of a dream that I had had many years before. It was a reoccurring dream during a time when I knew little about dreams. Many people in the Bible had dreams from God, but I could not imagine God giving me a dream.

After I had the dream about a dozen times, there was a change in the dream. Like most of my dreams, I could see myself. The last few times I had this dream, I was narrating the dream. I didn't know who I was talking to because I was the only person in the dream.

I asked Susan if she remembered my telling her the dream. She asked me why I wanted to remember the dream. I told her that there was a number in the dream that was significant, but I couldn't recall it.

The following is a description of the dream: I was going through a heavily wooded area on roller skates. There was just enough light on the path to see the curves and the bridges that went over the creeks. At the end of the path was a large house that was lit up. I entered through a door on the side of the house that was closest to the path. As I walked down the long, dimly lit hallway, I knew that I was supposed to go through the door at the end. All the doors in the hallway were shut and had a number. Before I saw my door, I knew the number that was on the door. When I opened the door, the light was so bright that I could not see anything. I did not hear anything in the room. Then the dream ended.

After I told Susan about the dream, she was excited. I asked God to give me the dream again. I knew the Lord was going to reveal the number to me, but I was impatient for the answer. Weeks went by and I still had not received the dream from the Lord.

Susan was looking for something in the study and found a three-ring binder that contained poems and stories that I had written many years before. As I reviewed the material, I was hopeful that I would find a description of the reoccurring dream. After several days, I found the description of my dream. The room number was included.

Recent Dreams

Even when I was a child, I knew that God was giving me dreams. I didn't understand that most dreams have symbols that need to be interpreted. When I shared my dreams with my friends, they were either scared or mystified along with me.

About ten years ago, I connected with friends who understand how God uses dreams to help His people. Since then, I have experienced periods when I received a dream from the Lord every night.

I often reread what I recorded. I'm amazed that my most recent dreams are helping me focus on the areas in my life that have been locked.

The following are a few of my recent dreams. Some of the details stick with me more than others.

I was in a large department store. I was looking for a large yellow boombox. I saw it on a shelf in the back of the store, so I went to get it. As I was coming around a corner, a large dog attacked me. It grabbed a hold of my left hand with its mouth and claws. I called for help, and a man came to assist me. He called off the dog and noticed that I needed medical attention. He made light of the fact that the dog attacked me, saying that it was doing its job. A man cut my shorts along my right leg. I was in so much pain that I wasn't looking at what he was doing. Then it felt like he was pulling on something inside of my body. There was a lot of pain associated with what he was doing. I couldn't figure out what he was doing, but I couldn't tell him to stop because I thought that he was taking care of me. When I woke up, I was still agonizing over the experience.

I was having difficulty tying my shoes. I was so frustrated that I said I would stay home.

Two wealthy men were taken into the hospital on a super stretcher.

People were traveling in ocean suits. They put a suit on that allowed them to go through the ocean quickly.

I took a shower.

An important key was hidden and then smuggled out of the royal home. The two political groups of the kingdom fussed and tried to manipulate things to their advantage.

Everyone was getting ready for the big move. Some were organizing their things, and others were taking some of their things home.

I was with a large group of people who were waiting for the buses to arrive. Most of the people wandered off. A woman knew where she was going, so several of us followed her.

A snowstorm was coming, and the weathermen predicted that there would be at least two feet.

I was looking at my computer and I saw a message that said that it was news. It appeared on the screen by itself. I did not initiate the request to see the news. Strange images appeared along with writing in different languages. I said to myself, "It is starting." I expected to see something that I could read in English or someone speaking to me in English, but that didn't happen.

145

I was walking home with Susan. There were large puddles of muddy water along the path. Susan slipped and landed in the water. I helped her up. She asked which leg got mud on it. I said both.

There were a lot of terrible accidents.

As I was driving along the highway, a friend asked me to pull over to help him. I did not record this dream. I recalled the dream as I was driving on a highway today.

The Interpretation

When my wife and I adopted our two children from Russia, we knew that there would be miscommunications. We knew little of the Russian language, and our children knew little of the English language. We eventually became a family that communicated because we all wanted to.

Initially, our son thought that the common language was going to be Russian. He thought that he was teaching us Russian while we were teaching him English. He didn't know there were so few people in the United States who knew Russian. As soon as that became evident to him, he quickly learned English. Our daughter had an advantage because her brother had recently gone through the communication challenges that she was going through.

When I finally realized that God was reaching out to me, I tried to learn the way He spoke. Like my daughter, I had older brothers and sisters who guided me through my communication challenges.

Although there are basic rules of grammar in God's language through dreams, He chooses vocabulary carefully for each one of His children. Our Heavenly Father knows us better than we know our children.

When I finally found the description of my reoccurring dream, I knew that the number on the door was significant. The number was twenty-three. The chapters and verses in the Bible were not included in the original writings. However, God knows that some of His children are intrigued with the use of numbers in the Bible.

146

God knew that I was familiar with Psalm 23 and that I would read it carefully when He showed me the number twenty-three.

While I was reading Psalm 23 recently, I recalled the challenges in my life at the time that God gave me the dream. God often uses dreams for multiple purposes and multiple times. I now believe that the dream was a reoccurring dream because I wasn't getting the message. It has become more significant as I am writing this book.

The Lord spoke to me through the dream before I knew that the number twenty-three was significant. When I was a child, I loved roller skates. My friends and I roller-skated up and down our street all summer long. Roller-skating is easier than walking if the ground is level or going downhill. My roller-skating through the wooded area in my dream was close to effortless.

The wooded area in my dream represented the dark times in my life. I wasn't into drugs or alcohol. My dark places were in my mind. I tried so hard to be what other people wanted me to be. I was almost a champion, but I came in second place. I won awards in high school, but I was not the valedictorian. I was an excellent software engineer, but someone else walked away with the award. I wanted to be the best, and people were expecting me to be the best. They never told me that I let them down, but I thought that I did.

If I went through the dark times with Him, it would have been as effortless as roller-skating. I don't know how I missed it when God was giving me the dreams. I knew that God is good, and He was watching over me, but I didn't give my struggles to Him. I thought I was good enough with a little bit of His help.

I grew up in a Baptist church. I was taught Bible stories, and I read the Bible myself. I did not know why God was giving me the dream, but I knew that the house at the end of the path represented heaven. One of the rooms was for me.

After I realized that God wanted me to meditate on Psalm 23, I saw the goodness of God much better. Going through the woods in my dream was representative of the valley of the shadow of death. All the times that I was disappointed, mistreated, or misunderstood, I was not alone. The Lord wanted to be my Shepherd, help me to lie down in green pastures, and lead me beside quiet waters. I wasn't being a good sheep. I was often the one who wandered off and found myself in dangerous territory where there were mean animals trying to destroy me.

The Application

"Papa, look at me!" My little girl was swinging higher and higher. I felt the need to tell her to not go so high.

When the little girl disappeared from the swing, a little boy appeared on the swing. "Daddy, look at me!"

I didn't want to open my eyes because the vision would go away. Sometimes, my thoughts create a vision. They seem so real. "Daddy, when you were a little boy, did you swing this high?"

When I was a little boy, I didn't have a swing. I rode on the swing at school. The teacher told us that we were swinging too high. I wanted to swing higher than anybody else, but I wasn't allowed to.

My emotions were starting to overtake me, so I opened my eyes.

I wondered if I should include this vision. It is part of my story, so I'm including it.

When I was roller-skating at home, nobody told me that I was going too fast or taking the curves too quickly. I loved to roller-skate. All my friends had roller skates too. That's why I was on roller skates in my reoccurring dream. God was telling me that He was releasing me. It was OK for teachers and parents to be concerned about children. Children tend to go wild and do dangerous things. However, I did not have to live my life in a way that pleased everyone.

Why was I in the woods? Why did I have to go over creeks? Why was I alone?

One dream isn't going to solve all my problems or help me through all my challenges. God promised to help me deal with hurts and disappointments. They act like dungeons and jail cells. Even after

I learned to deal with unreasonable expectations, they came back to haunt me again.

God speaks in different ways, but He always speaks. When I am listening, the locks disappear.

CHAPTER 20

Evidence of God's Goodness

Sometimes, I think I'm doing just fine. The only reason to ask God for help is that I believe that He is always good. My solution is just OK, but His is always amazing.

I Was Available to Help Susan During Her Times of Greatest Need.

Susan had heart bypass surgery. When the staff saw me sleeping on a couch near her room, they moved Susan into a suite in the hospital. There was a room for family members to relax and sleep on a pullout bed. I slept on that bed for several days. When it was time for her to be transferred to a critical rehab center, there was confusion about which of her medical plans would be primary and which would be secondary. She was covered by Medicare and private insurance through my company. My small company was growing, and it was difficult to know when the insurance would switch from Medicare being primary to Blue Cross being primary. The hospital seemed to be OK with it, but there was confusion at the rehabilitation facility that Susan was going to. Dawn and Don, owners of my company, were on their vacation. Dawn often works even when she's on vacation. I told her my problem, and she spent a significant amount of time helping to work through the medical insurance problem.

Susan was able to recover from her heart surgery much faster than the doctors expected.

Susan was brought to the hospital because of the pain she had in her abdomen. They quickly determined that her appendix needed to be taken out. This was very unusual for a person of her age. The surgery was done almost immediately. The surgeon said that he had never seen an appendix that was in that bad shape. He expected that it would burst and pour poison into her body. The doctor never said this, but I concluded that it was a miracle.

On several occasions, Susan had a medical emergency while she was at home. The Lord arranged for me to be there to help her get the medical attention that she needed.

The clearest example of me being available for Susan was the time that she had meningitis. I was planning to go out to dinner with some of the men of our church that evening. Before I went to dinner, I stopped by the house to see how Susan was doing. Susan had chopped vegetables that she was going to eat for dinner. When I arrived, she was sitting in a chair, and I thought that she was just relaxing. I found out quickly that there was something happening that neither of us knew enough to diagnose. I called 911, and the EMTs brought her to the hospital. Meningitis is serious. Depending on the type you have, it can kill you within twenty-four hours. If I had gone directly to the restaurant, it would've been several hours before I returned home. Those hours were critical for providing the medical treatment Susan needed.

God Used Susan to Release Me.

I never wanted to leave Susan alone. It was hard for me when I was working. The Lord provided a job with a flexible work schedule. When it became evident that I was not going to be able to continue with a full-time job, I retired. Even when Susan was in the hospital or a rehabilitation center, I wanted to be with her as much as the facility would allow. There were times when she would not have been given adequate attention if I were not available to do nonmedical things for her.

I did not want to do anything else when I could be available to help Susan. Susan would say something like, "I don't want to hold you back." Sometimes she would elaborate, but mostly that's all she said.

On September 30, 2023, Susan was in a rehab center recovering from a stroke. I was planning to go to a prophetic seminar on that day. When I visited Susan in the morning before the seminar started, I decided that I wasn't going to go to the seminar. When I told Susan, she said, "You must go to the seminar. It's important."

After talking with Susan for a few minutes, I changed my mind and went to the seminar. That seminar was fundamental to what God wanted me to do in this season. I had no idea that Susan would die soon. Susan asked me when she could return home. The Lord used Susan to convince me to go to the seminar. Susan died ten days later in the ICU. I went to another seminar a month later. That seminar was also foundational for what the Lord is calling me to do.

God Provided a Way for Me to Be in Frederick.

In the summer of 2020, the COVID pandemic was in full swing. Many businesses were closed or limited significantly. In large government workspaces, most government employees stayed home, while some contractors worked with limited staff. I worked forty hours every other week. However, my employer arranged for funds to be available to pay all the employees a full-time salary.

Susan and I were planning to move. We looked at several places in the Gaithersburg area. We could not find a place that was appropriate for our needs. Our real estate agent found a house close to Frederick. The mortgage company did not believe me when I said that my full salary was guaranteed by my company. The president of my company wrote a letter that convinced the mortgage company to give us a mortgage for our new house.

In the same week that we signed the contract for our new house, our church announced that they were starting a meeting in the Frederick area. This was confirmation that the Lord was sending us to Frederick.

When the leadership of our church announced that they were reorganizing, they indicated that the one and only meeting would be in Montgomery County. Susan and I ask the Lord if we should stay in Frederick. We did not sense that the Lord was saying that we should move, and we did not know if we should stay with our current church or look for one in the Frederick area.

Shortly after Susan died, I asked the Lord if He wanted me to find a church in the Frederick area. My heart was still for the Frederick people, but it was becoming increasingly difficult for me. The Lord told me that I was too far away from the vision that He had given Susan and me.

After several months, the Lord directed me to a church that is primarily focused on Frederick County. Every week, I receive additional confirmation that the Lord has placed me in this community of believers.

CHAPTER 21

Permanently Free

I love great mysteries, but my wife always wanted to know what happened in the end. If she liked the end of the story, then she spent the time reading the whole story and enjoyed it.

If you are like my wife and skipped to the end, I trust that this chapter will be sufficient for you to decide to read the whole book. Knowing the answer is helpful; however, experiencing it is so much greater.

Over the years, I kept a lot of memorabilia. Unfortunately, they don't help me because I don't know where most of the stuff is. I still have dozens of boxes in my basement from four years ago when I moved here with my wife.

The grace of God was always upon my life. I was never lacking a good friend. Sometimes, I thought I didn't have one, but I did. My best friend over the longest period was my wife. I am hoping to find more things that remind me of the personal interaction she had with me. Our conversations were never recorded, but she always found a way to give me a reminder of who she was to me.

I try to be careful so that I will not make an idol of something that my wife gave me. My greatest treasure right now is a birthday card that Susan made for me. I don't know what year it was, but the content is profound. The front of the card has a picture of a man sitting on a bench looking at the clouds. The scripture is Psalm 40:1 and 40:3-5. The psalmist was waiting patiently for the Lord.

The only thing Susan wrote in her hand was, "Waiting patiently with you to see your every prayer fulfilled. Love you more every day!" She signed the card, "Susan (Sweet Pea)." Sweet Pea was my special name for her. On the back of the card, Susan created a small picture of President Trump with a party hat. The caption says, "Let's make your birthday great again."

My mother had cancer for five years when I was a teenager. We cared for her and prayed for her. I could not imagine anyone being more loving than she was. I could not imagine putting more of my heart into caring for somebody. When my mother died, I felt like I was thrown into a dungeon, but I did not stay there long. My family and friends pulled me out because there was no lock on the door.

I waited and waited, and waited some more. I knew that I would be loved again. Fifteen years later, I married my best friend. Every year, our love increased.

When Susan was taken to the ICU, she told the doctor that her husband would make all the decisions for her. If I were locked in a dungeon, I would not have been able to make the right decisions. There was peace in my heart. I knew where it came from, but I also knew that I didn't deserve it. Others have been in a similar situation and believed that God would give them peace, but they don't have the same testimony that I do. I don't know why, but I know the One who knows.

When I was passed over for a technical award, my coworkers encouraged me. They said that I deserved the award and were glad that I was on their team. I was thrown into a dungeon. Before I hit the bottom, I felt a rope around my waist. They pulled me back up. I gladly gave up the $10,000 award, believing that my provision was not coming from my employer but from the Lord. When Susan and I decided to adopt children, we did not have the money. We knew the One who provides, and He did.

When my pastor told me that I was wasting my life because I wasn't married, I was thrown into a dungeon. When I climbed out, the sun was shining, and I could feel the presence of the Holy Spirit as He encouraged me. My neighbor invited me to his church. I knew something special was happening in my life. I met Susan there, and we married four years later.

I always wanted to be a champion. One of my favorite songs when I was growing up has the line, "We are the champions of the world" (Songwriter: Freddie Mercury, We Are the Champions lyrics © Queen Music Limited).

I wondered what it would be like to be a champion of the world or my little piece of the world. Each time I got close to being a champion, someone threw me into jail and locked the door. But I didn't stay there long. The grace of God always unlocked the door and set me free. It was easy for me to get thrown back into that jail because its lock had not been removed.

Even today, I struggle with a desire to be the best. I wasn't the best son. I wasn't the best brother. I wasn't the best employee. I wasn't the best husband. I wasn't the best friend. But I know the One who is.

Jesus is the best Son. He is the best big brother to me. He shows me how to follow the Father. He is the best husband for His bride. He's the best friend anyone could ever have.

If you ask Him, He will save you from your sins. He will be your best friend too.

"So if the Son sets you free, you will be free indeed"(John 8:36 ESV).

ABOUT THE AUTHOR

Richard Kirby Payne has used his gift of storytelling to entertain, encourage, and teach since he was young. His writing is inspired by his focus on God's love and his personal experiences. Payne, who is active in his church, currently resides in New Market, Maryland. *Remove the Lock: Become Permanently Free* is his second book.

Printed in the United States
by Baker & Taylor Publisher Services